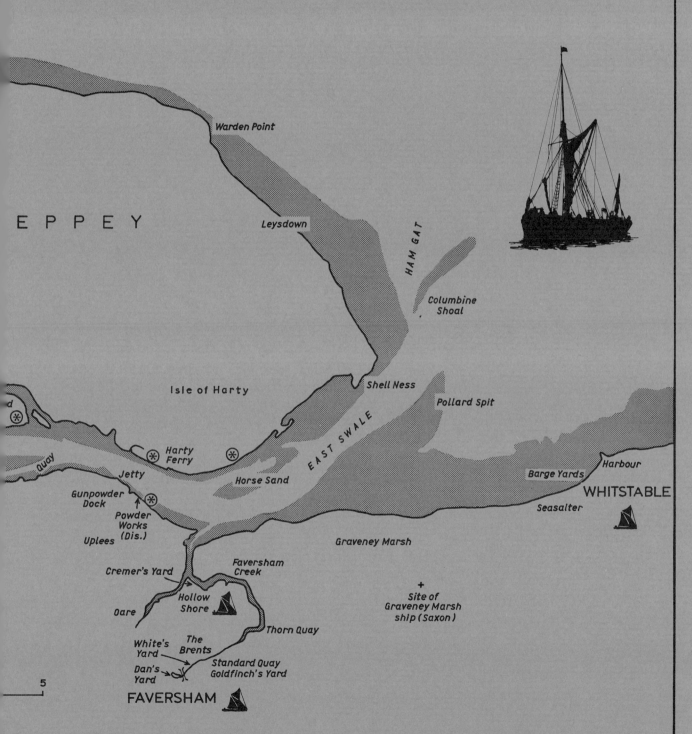

E P P E Y

Warden Point

Leysdown

HAM GAT

Columbine Shoal

Isle of Harty

Shell Ness

Pollard Spit

EAST SWALE

Horse Sand

Barge Yards — Harbour

WHITSTABLE

Seasalter

Harty Ferry

Jetty

Gunpowder Dock

Powder Works (Dis.)

Uplees

Quay

Graveney Marsh

+
Site of Graveney Marsh ship (Saxon)

Cremer's Yard

Faversham Creek

Oare

Hollow Shore

Thorn Quay

White's Yard

The Brents

Dan's Yard

Standard Quay
Goldfinch's Yard

FAVERSHAM

5

A E Reed.

May 1983

ITEM 12.

SPRITS'L

By the same author
A History of Faversham Sailing Barges
Sailing Coasters of Kent (In preparation)

Richard-Hugh Perks

SPRITS'L

A portrait of sailing barges and sailormen

Written in collaboration with
Patricia O'Driscoll and Alan Cordell

Conway Maritime Press
Greenwich

First published in Great Britain 1975
by Conway Maritime Press Limited

7 Nelson Road Greenwich London SE10

Copyright © Richard-Hugh Perks 1975

ISBN 0 85177 073 8

To "J"

Designed by Martin Treadway

Text set in 12pt Times New Roman by
Lexis Typesetting Co Ltd
London SE24 OHW

Printed and bound by Page Bros, Norwich

Contents

Photographs

In a number of instances it has proved impossible to trace the original holders of photographs reproduced as many of them have been passed down from hand to hand and are now in collections. I have indicated where possible these owners and the holders of the collections from which they have come.

Introduction

Wide, opaque wastes of shoal waters speckled with tints of pale sand and cloudy silt; rough, hardy beacons, withies and scarred buoys sounding cold chimes; wavering shapes hull-down on a hazy sea; and scouring tides flecked up by cats paws of wind, whispering and gurgling through the swatchways. These are the old Eastcoast-roads—the sailing ground of the sprits'l barges.

Once I attempted in a lecture to define what sprits'l barges were all about, why people were interested in them, why there was this fascination for them. I found it difficult in my own mind to frame any adequate answer, as this interest is not just confined to what the barge is, or was; neither, I have decided, is it restricted entirely to the barges themselves.

Let me try to explain.

The fundamental interest exists perhaps because in the barge there was a greater opportunity to observe commercial sail under working conditions than there was in other classes of vessel. The sail enthusiast was not permitted to enjoy the sight of a barque or fully-rigged ship at sea under sail for more than a few brief moments, passing ships, no more, and only the crews of similar craft could see them hard-pressed in the Southern latitudes. For the watcher on the shore had to be content if he saw a barque under reduced canvas making landfall, or under tow, for such big ships were seldom able to sail freely within sight of land, and when in port they might be hid behind greyed, brick walls amid the institutional life of dockland—to which entry for many was prohibited. The coasting brigs and schooners required sea-room for their passages, so the enthusiast was fortunate if he could achieve more than a fleeting intimacy with them.

With the sprits'l barge this was so very different. Everyone knew the London river barge and could, if they wished, share in the full and complete picture, and most Londoners had familiar knowledge of them. Pick up a book on London, many have illustrations of barges in them: "See, that's a Thames barge; you know, we used to see them down off Southend Pier. Not many of 'em left, now." And the barge was not just a part of London; her home was in the tideway, yet it was also at the small, Georgian townships of the Kent, Essex and Suffolk coasts, and the little havens at the heads of tiny gutways, which were called ports only because they possessed a mill and a wharf or farm landing. The barge was accessible to all and if you wanted to make a trip aboard one then there were plenty of Masters willing to oblige. She could be watched without leaving the comfort of the shore, from any number of vantage points along the East Coast, actually performing the task she was designed to do—working the tideway under full canvas, creeping close into banks and coastlines that her deeper hulled sisters had to steer away from.

The enthusiast was able to watch and photograph her from such a close proximity both at sea and in the river, that she now enjoys the distinction of being one of the most carefully documented of all craft, and certainly the most photographed.

Her numerical advantage, which accounts for her casual appearance in so many photographs and snap shots, made her an accepted part to the background of the East coast ports. Take away the barge and any port has lost something of its character. In fact, if the sprits'l barge had not been favoured with such fortunate surroundings then the enthusiasm for her would be lessened, for there is a certain influence about the barge ports; one takes pleasure in visiting them to walk around their enticing waterfronts, to view their fine old buildings and churches, conscious of their great historical connection. Thus, the enjoyment of making a passage by barge is added to considerably by the actual visit to a port, by being able to appreciate, for example, when rounding Herring Point the still, beautiful panorama of the Maldon waterside. How much more exciting this than say approaching Grimsby!

The beauty of East Anglia is not something instantly apparent. It cannot be opened up like a picture book to which a reader can say "Oh" or "Ah" to. It is so wide that it is hidden, and is only found slowly and delicately, like the ultimate pleasure experienced when you discover that you like eating oysters. It lies in the gently undulating hills, in the incredible brightness of the skies, in the grey tints which inlay every colour in the seascape, and in the great travelling clouds. It is here and under these conditions where the simple grace and ease of a sprits'l barge moving against this backcloth first attracts a real understanding for them.

Comparable with a dray horse or a steam locomotive a barge is an expression of powerful energy. Understandably, it is hard not to feel a thrill surging through one at the sight of such a craft cracking on canvas, confidently working her way to wind'ard through shoal water; brilliant dark canvas, pale ochre spars, absolutely alive with colour. Here is sound, the most exciting element of the sea—the rush of water gurgling at a forefoot overlaid with the clank of a pawl, and the clatter of patent blocks— a sound and a sense capable of imbuing any watcher worth his (or her) salt with a complete feeling of restlessness.

Watch a barge pick up from a deserted anchorage. Catch the preliminary clank of windlass pawls, as her crew wind the anchor out of the mud; notice the halt, and then the sharply rung chinks as chain falls on chain to be fleeted until finally the anchor breaks free of the ground. Blocks creak as tops'l sheet is drawn out to the sprit end and the headstick creeps up the topmast pole. Fores'l is set, followed by the sudden grating of wire round a drum when the mainbrail is unleashed: a series of thumps as the traveller flogs against the vang falls; then the final clank of chain as the anchor stock comes awash to the low murmuring from the hull as it breaks free on the tide. Watch, while the rudder catches the flow and the barge hangs up in stays until sails fill and she bears away.

These are senses, sight and sound and feeling which appeal so much to the lover of sail, whose contribution has enabled the sprits'l barge to continue in a private capacity after cessation of her working life; but the barge also had a particularly strong appeal for those who sailed them professionally. Picture the barge as she sometimes was in trade—mains'l half brailed, tops'l rucked home and fores'l straining against its horse, water up to the iron band with the hull juddering and heeling to meet the sea— and you will understand something about the difficult conditions under which the sailormen operated. To them the answer I think was job satisfaction, found in the compensation of leading an independent life.

But this is still not a complete answer. For this fascination we derive from sprits'l barges is more than just the preservation of former working craft, or the enjoyment associated with their historical connections. Get interested in them and you suddenly find yourself inexplicably caught up in an entire pattern of life.

In trade the sprits'l barge fulfilled an important economic function. Historically she brought cargoes of cereals, sand, cement, bricks and stack upon stack of hay and straw, to satisfy the ever increasing demands of London town, returning with the commodities that the East Coast towns required. It was a life of infinite variety: working up through Thames bridges under oars or bridge sails; lying idle on the buoys waiting for work, sometimes for weeks upon end; rolling windbound at anchor in an estuary mouth; setting sail, hard pressed in a seaway; entering unlit channels by night; and blowing up to berths in impossibly narrow creeks. It was unloading into horsedrawn carts, brought across the sands or hard mud; being loaded with bricks and cement and straw by

Plate 1. The author (L) with two of his former Skippers, Captain "Bill" Hamilton (C) of *Repertor* and Captain George Eastland of *Convoy*. (Picture East Kent Gazette).

gangers at isolated landings: then it was back up with another delivery; past sea-marks with exciting names; through Thames reaches bordering drab and ugly foreshores and so into Dockland, to be greeted by the familiar hail - "Hey, Sailorman!"

This book, then, is brief pictures of a working life, of how it came into being and of the people who were associated with it—not so much for what they did but how they came to do it and why: and with Patricia O'Driscoll and Alan Cordell photographs have been chosen from our collections to illustrate the barge in some of these aspects of her life. By strange fortune not only do a healthy number of sprits'l barges exist today, but with them many of the old skills and crafts which went into the making of this extraordinary way of life afloat have been preserved, and revived by men who are still able to cut sails and shape spars for them. Writing this book has given me the opportunity to record how some of these tasks are performed.

I am grateful to those who have allowed me to freely choose illustrations from their collections, and to those who have let me sail with them over the last 21 years and take photographs from their barges, especially to Alan and Lena Reekie of *Ironsides* and Martin Loverock of *Lady Gwynfred*.

In compiling the text I acknowledge the assistance given by my friends Roger Minter, who has compiled so much on the history of the Colne; Don Wright and Captain Charles Simmons at Maldon; Nigel Halsey who with Claude Meeson researched deeply into the Crouch and Roach histories of their two families; Mrs Huffle whose recollections of the stack trade are invaluable; Mrs Muriel Gentry, daughter of the late James Arthur Woodward, who helped me with details of barge building; Vera Vandervord at Leigh-on-Sea; Frank Willmott at Rainham; Tom Redshaw and "Chippy" Wood at Milton; John Wills of Wills & Packham at Sittingbourne who helped me on the brickmaking industry; William Bunting and Captain Charles Frake at Faversham; and to the various members of the Society for Spritsail Barge Research who over the years have helped me with historical detail on sailing barges: Captains Bill Hamilton and Bill Blake; the Society Historian, Joseph Hines, who also provided the material for the index; Anthony Ellis; Robert Simper and Edward Perry. Also I would like to thank James Howgego and David Webb of the Guildhall Library and the Bishopsgate Institute respectively for allowing me to use the facilities of their extensive documentary collections; to Tony Winter of Crescent Shipping who kindly read the manuscript through and, last but not least, Rod Fraser who drew the maps for text and endpapers.

Finally, I am especially grateful to Patricia and Alan for agreeing to assist me in producing this book and allowing me to draw on their knowledge and experiences, and to Jenefer who put up with having our cottage littered with photographs and manuscripts.

Richard-Hugh Perks
Eastling,
Faversham,
1975.

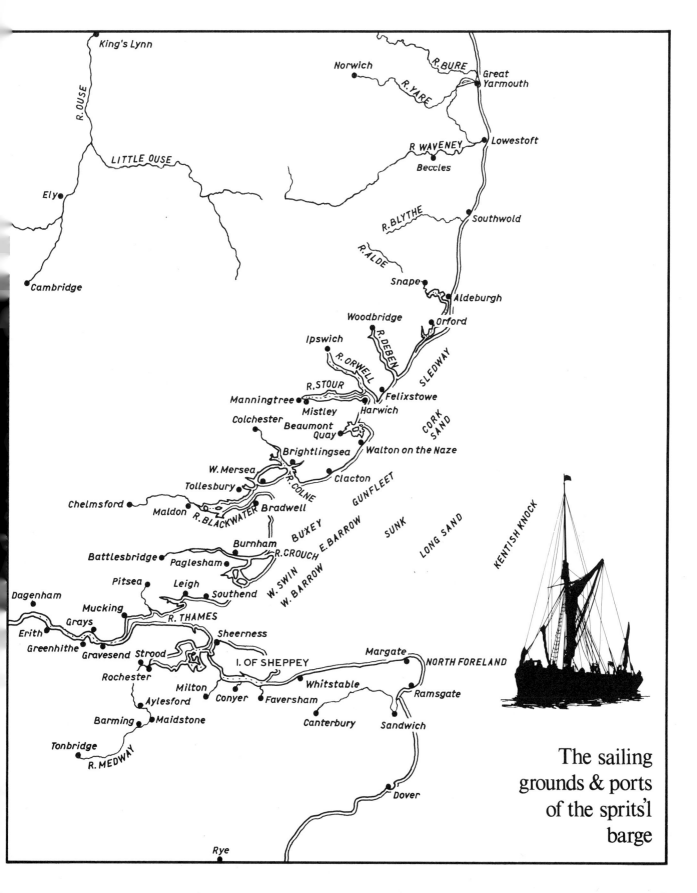

King's Lynn

R. OUSE

R.BURE

Norwich

R.YARE

Great
Yarmouth

LITTLE OUSE

R WAVENEY

Lowestoft

Beccles

Ely

R.BLYTHE

Southwold

R.ALDE

Cambridge

Snape

Aldeburgh

Woodbridge

Orford

Ipswich

R.DEBEN

R.ORWELL

SLEDWAY

R.STOUR

Manningtree

Felixstowe

Mistley

Harwich

Colchester

Beaumont
Quay

CORK
SAND

Brightlingsea

Walton on the Naze

W. Mersea

Clacton

Tollesbury

R.COLNE

GUNFLEET

Chelmsford

R.BLACKWATER Bradwell

Maldon

SUNK

LONG SAND

BUXEY

KENTISH KNOCK

Burnham

R.CROUCH E.BARROW

Battlesbridge

Paglesham

W. SWIN

Pitsea

Leigh

W. BARROW

Dagenham

Southend

Mucking

Grays

R. THAMES

Erith

Sheerness

Greenhithe

Margate

Gravesend Strood

NORTH FORELAND

Rochester

I. OF SHEPPEY

Milton

Ramsgate

Aylesford

Conyer

Whitstable

Barming

Faversham

Maidstone

Sandwich

Canterbury

Tonbridge

R. MEDWAY

Dover

Rye

The sailing
grounds & ports
of the sprits'l
barge

Chapter I
A HISTORY OF THE SPRITS'L BARGE

The history of the East Anglian coastline is a deep and exciting one which back from earliest recorded times was immeasurably linked with mercantile trade. This coast was never an easy one to navigate and its rivers lie behind banks of sand and mud, while parts of the coastline are below the high water level. Always men have struggled to dig and maintain harbours, to embank the sea-walls, and to convert the marshes into rich, fertile lands. Even in 1322 we learn that Adam de Barling was obliged to raise a wall on his own grounds to keep out the inundations of the sea; while later parts of the Dengie Hundred were embanked by the volatile Henry Bate, Bradwell's "Fighting Parson." Sometime Editor of the Morning Post, duellist, prisoner, foremost agriculturalist of his day, he became the Reverend Sir Henry Bate Dudley, surely one of the most colourful characters to emerge from the 18th century. Over 200 years before Dudley, one Ralph Breeder had given money for the repairing of the haven and channels and bridges

Plate 2. Rough, hardy beacons, withies and scarred buoys. *Millie* **off the Wallet Spitway Buoy. (Picture Patricia O'Driscoll).**

Plate 3. As common in books on barges as barges were themselves. A tops'l barge of the 1860's seen at the Atroyal Brewery Wharf around 1880. The old wooden Putney bridge is in the rearground. Note the diminutive transom and extremely long rudder. (Picture by Courtesy of the Executors of the Late E. P. Olney).

Plate 4. When barges were "two-a-penny" . . . a fleet of barges and other craft off Greenwich before the turn of the century. The craft in the foreground has rucked her tops'l, a traditional method of reducing canvas in a blow. Her narrow transom identifies her as having been built at the Swale ports in the 1860's. Note her flat profile in comparison with the heavily sheered lines of the craft in front. (Picture M. A. Farnham Collection).

at Maldon. But creeks silt up, sandbanks shift and fortunes change.

This is a proud and racy history. Men like Lionel de Bradenham of Langenhoe, possibly the greatest villain to come out of Essex history, who among other exploits attempted to misappropriate part of the Royalty of the Colne by enclosing the Geedons with piles in 1362, played a part in it, as did the mournful Arthur Young, partially blind, who wrote such valuable accounts of East Anglian rural conditions. But to define history is not simply to consider great deeds, battles, heroes and villains, but also the day to day experiences of ordinary people who won their livings from the land or the sea. From these accounts have come down to us knowledge of how men lived in the days when Eastern England relied on its waterways for its trade and very existence, and when reputations were being built up for the great coastal towns which became the sleepy ports we know today.

The sprits'l barge was a product of an age of adaptation and by the time that craft of this rig were first seen down the Essex coast, William Bentall had marketed his renowned Goldhanger Plough, while fertile and inventive minds had designed the steam threshing engine. The sprits'l barge fitted well into this age and soon became the most significant feature of the seaboard.

Barges of course were only a small part of this history, but quite an important one as they were the most convenient means of transporting bulk cargoes cheaply. If you were a brickmaker in Woodbridge, a hay and straw merchant at Maldon or a corn factor at Milton you would have owned one or more barges to carry your products to whichever wharf was nearest to their destination. The barge's shallow draft coupled with a rig that was more simple to handle than that of other contemporary craft made her a very versatile carrier, able to work both to the heads of the narrower channels which were unreached by other hulls, and to the deep water ports up and down the coast. But her greatest multiformity lay in her ability to be owned on one hand by a group of shareholders, and on the other by a company, some of whom owned fleets of over one hundred barges.

The principal owners were manufacturers or merchants who kept barges in the way they now keep motor lorries. These men were usually the largest local employers of labour, so that in almost every port the working population came to be involved in barges in one way or another. The history of the sprits'l barge, then, involved the men and sometimes women who worked in the fields, mills, yards, as well as the specialists who tended the barges, the "gangers" who loaded-up, the "muddies" and "sandies" who dug these minerals from the foreshores, the "hufflers" who piloted the craft, blacksmiths, shipwrights, block and sailmakers and the barge crews themselves. It was a very ordinary history.

If we could go back in time and view the coastal panorama of only 70 years ago, when the barge was enjoying the heyday of her era, we would find, for example, that the sprit rig predominated among the great variety of craft to be found at the East Anglian ports. Working out of the Swale and Medway creeks would be the

Plate 5. Creeping close into banks and coastlines. . . . Off Hollow Shore. (Picture the Author).

Plate 6. The still beautiful panorama of the Maldon waterfront. . . . In the centre Cook & Woodward's yard under St. Mary's tower, on the immediate left a barge is under construction on the bank. To the left of this are two Victorian bathing machines. A stack barge is coming away from the Hythe, right, and in the extreme right is John Howard's barge yard, with one of his Maldoner's in the foreground. (Picture "The Dustbin Collection").

brick and cement barges, some of them stump rigged, that is without topmasts, crowded against the quays of Lower Halstow and Otterham where there was a high concentration of brickfields. By far the greatest number of barges were owned in these particular waters, and it must have been a great sight to see them coming down through the Estuary off the Medway mouth. The Faversham craft would carry on "round the Island" and enter the East Swale through the Ham Gat, while Milton craft went up past Queenborough and through the narrow Kingsferry Bridge. Over towards the north shore of the Estuary would be the Essex and Suffolk craft making for the West Swin, and with them would be the larger coasters and ketch barges going way down the coast, whose course would take them to the seaward side of the Gunfleet Sands. We would have found barges fetching across the Overland Route, down through the Gore to Margate or the Foreland; lying in the shelter of Yarmouth Roads or the Downs; tied up at almost every port between Hull and Newlyn; and making landfalls off the Tyne, Elbe, Scheldt, Seine and Somme.

Fortunately many families treasured their connections with barges and have kept old photographs, papers and other items concerned with their associations, while there are elderly men and women who can remember days when the quays up and down the coast were

Plate 7. The simple grace and ease of a sprits'l barge. (Picture Author's Collection).

Plate 8. An expression of powerful energy . . . *Westmoreland* romping in towards the shore. (Picture Mike Hicks).

Plate 9. Cracking on canvas, confidently working her way to wind'ard in shoal water. (Picture the Author).

crowded with schooners, smacks, the occasional cutter, brig, barque and the ever present sprits'l barge: times when ports the size of Maldon boasted over 150 head of trading sail. These recollections coupled with contemporary records, registers and newspaper accounts make up this panorama for us.

With the social benefits we enjoy today it is difficult to realise that there ever was a time when the working day might be from six in the morning to past seven in the evening, and when every member of the family was expected to contribute something by way of income. From an early age boys in the brick ports were employed in the evenings to sift through the mounds of "London Mixture," graduating around the age of eleven to become Third Hands afloat. On retirement many former Masters went back afloat as Mates or became watchmen . . . all had to work. At Maldon, I am told there was even a blind sailmaker, who for a while worked for Saddler.

Labour then was cheap, and ships were more valuable than men. Yet almost without exception the "old timers" I have spoken to recall these days with fondness.

Each had their favourite barge, and would contest the merits of one build over another, arguing which was the most attractive, which the more sea-kindly.

Then as now the most attractive to look at might have been the stack barges, the hay and straw carriers, like *Rose* which John Howard built for Charles Hawes in 1880. They were of shallow draft, beamy, and had exquisitely carved and delicate shaped transoms, as you can see from the picture of *Rose* and from the pictures of other Howard barges *Ready* and the mill barges *Ethel Maud* and *Saltcote Belle. Jachin, Hyacinth* and *Violet* were among

a number of Howard barges to be named after flowers. The bow and quarter badge scroll work incorporated the design of the particular flower.

No two barges looked the same, even to the practiced eye, even though the builder embodied certain recognisable characteristics in all his craft, and design varied from port to port according to the type of work a barge was required for. Howard's barges were lightly built with weak quarters but had good sailing qualities, and *Ethel Maud*, for example, was very easy to sail light laden, even if she did slap water on her hatches when she was deep.

The Essex and Suffolk builders paid great attention to shape and ornamentation, and their larger craft which went coasting often had some very beautiful scroll-work. Their duties required them to be powerfully built, able to ride seas rather than plough through them incorporating graceful sheerlines, higher rails, sometimes with bow boards, and coamings to keep their cargoes dry. Compare the photographs of the stack barges with those of the Ipswich built *Spinaway C* of 57 tons and the Harwich built *Centaur* of 60 tons.

The greatest number of barges to be built, however, were those from London River and North Kent of which many were designed for estuary work as low, flat, long-chined little craft, with a minimum of sheer and sparse adornment. Some were built with dimensions of a 14-foot beam on a 76-foot hull, the maximum size which permitted entry into London's canal system.

The estuary or river barge, sailed either tops'l or stump rigged, was generally speedy and would handle well in confined waters. The stump rig is illustrated in Plate 31. The sprit was high-peaked, and as the stumpy's great area of mains'l proved hard to control in a blow barges like *Yieldsted* were later re-rigged with topmasts.

Seventy years ago it would have been possible to stand at the cross-roads of marine history when sail had already stepped down to steam, and still find afloat almost every type of barge which had contributed to the evolution of this rig. There were on one hand the then modern coasters (although Everard's and Paul's big steel coasters had yet to be built), on the other there were round or bluff bowed barges, swim-headers, while the diligent among barge spotters of the day would have come across various gaff or booms'l rigs, and a few, precious examples of the cutters, chalk barges and sloops which preceded the era of the sprits'l barge.

The estuary chalk barge of the late 18th century may, I think, be considered as the immediate ancestor of the sprits'l barge, although we might perhaps not recognise it as such. They were built swim-headed, and budget-sterned, with a hull length of around 45 to 50 feet, similar to that of a Thames lighter except that they were decked over, usually with a single hatch but sometimes twin-hatched, and had crudely built after cabins under raised cabin tops which stretched out from quarter board to quarter board. They would not in this period have set mizzens. Plate 22 shows the old *Admiral Blake*, whose remains are the only surviving example of this type. Built with a single hatch and a swim bow she ultimately became a gaff rigged mud barge, lying for many years at Queenborough before finally being hulked in Shepherd's Creek in the

Plate 10. Brilliant dark canvas, pale ochre spars, absolutely alive with colour . . . Sailormen brought-up. (Picture Patricia O'Driscoll).

Plate 11. The traveller flogs against the vang falls . . . (Picture Patricia O'Driscoll).

Plate 12. Watch while the rudder catches the flow and the barge hangs up in stays until the wind fills her sails and she bears away . . . an "ironpot" off Southend around 1950. She is wearing a device in her tops'l. (Picture C. Beazley).

Plate 13. The hull juddering and heeling to meet the sea. (Picture Les Arnold).

early 1950's. She is approximately 180 to 190 years old.

Coastal passage work up until the early years of the 19th century was in the hands of the larger cutter and sloop rigged barges which often maintained regular hoy services. The lesser of these were in fact only slightly larger versions of the chalk and hay barges, and again were built swim-headed, but those which worked outside the confines of the estuary appear to have been stem-headed. A small number of these were still at work towards the end of the 19th century, and incredibly one or two survived until just before the Great War. One, the *Good Intent* had a deep, rounded bow and stern, a chubby hull with lofty mast, and long, overhanging boom. The illustration of her was probably taken at Whitstable where she was owned by the Collard family.

I have no evidence that these early coasting hoys were ever re-rigged as sprits'l barges. I think their hull shape would have been unsuitable, although it is probable that some of the early swim-headed sloops were re-rigged as spritties. But some hung onto their old rigs throughout their working lives, and Vandervord's *Royal Oak* built booms'l rigged at Limehouse in 1798 was still carrying that rig when a record tersely noted in 1894 that she had been found to be unsound and was dismantled.

Sprits'l barges had been built in small numbers on the Thames and in North Kent in the years immediately prior to 1800, but these were only more substantial versions of the existing chalk barges. It would appear, then, to have been around the 1820's that larger hulls were designed to be fitted with the sprit rig for passage work, a period of perhaps 20 years passing before this rig became common in Suffolk and Norfolk. These first, true sprits'l barges were tops'l rigged, mounted mizzens on the rudder heads, some carrying bowsprits and even square fores'ls in the manner of the cutters they were soon to usurp. Registers show that such craft were nearly all built on the Thames; Limehouse, Rotherhithe, Southwark, Lambeth, Battersea, Chelsea and even towns as far up river as Reading and Pangbourne are recorded as their birthplaces, while down in the estuary mouth they were built at Sittingbourne and Faversham. One of these was the noted Queenborough hoy *Royal Frederick*.

Few good photographs exist of the early swim-headed rig. One of the best of these is W. H. Fox Talbot's view of two such craft near old Hungerford Bridge, taken around 1845. It can be seen that the main masts are raked forward. The swim bow is highlighted in the powerful watercolour, believed to be the work of Joshua Taylor, of a stumpy off Sheerness in about 1850. She carries a raised bow rail above which can be seen the bitts of her hand spike windlass. Mains'ls of this period were hooped to their masts.

It was during the late 1840's that the round bow gained popularity as the barge became more of a sea-going craft. Stems were raked and one of the more interesting craft to catch the eye of the pin-hole camera was one of these, the stumpy *Alfred*, which I judge to be the one built at Bankside in 1847 and later in the ownership of George Smeed. Her wood stayfall blocks are considerably more massive than the later metal ones. The headrope and shrouds would have been of hemp. I am amused by the

Plate 14. Fores'l straining against the horse . . . *Gold Belt* (ex *Orion*) "down Swin". (Picture John Corello).

variety of dress worn by the persons on board. The tarred bowler hat and the cheesecutter were the accepted forms of head-gear, and although the latter is still frequently used the bowler has been discontinued; however I have been known to wear my City bowler during exceptional downpours, and I am told that a gentleman member of the Thames Barge Sailing Club was once seen wearing a sporting alternative in the form of an undersealed trilby!

Illustrations of craft from the mid part of the 19th century show that hulls were largely undecorated, even to the extent that on some barges the name was only painted and not carved on the bow and stern. In the days of tiller steering carving was reserved for the tiller bar where the name of the barge or the initials of the owner might be set into a panel close to the rudder head. Bow and quarter badges did not become fashionable until the 1860's and I believe

Plate 15. The coming and going with ships on the tide . . . the Upper Pool in the 1890's, crowded with steamers, brigs, hoys, lighters and carrier ships. Twelve sprits'l barges are brought up near the Tower. Custom House is in the rearground. (Picture Bishopsgate Institute).

that Howard's *Surprise* was the first barge to bear scroll-work on her transom.

The sprit rig and barge hull proved unsuitable for long coastal passages, so from the middle of the 19th century another form of barge evolved, the ketch barge, or boomie. The hulls were powerful, being akin to the ketch or schooner above the waterline and were fitted with gaff sails. The illustration of Cook & Woodward's Maldon yard shows a boomie barge on the blocks.

For a period sail and steam had run in uneasy competition; but although iron steamers came to replace many of the North Country fore-and-afters, especially in the coal and timber trades, generally sea trade was losing ground to the locomotive. Towards the turn of the century there were still conventional brigs and schooners to be seen sailing out of the larger East Anglian ports—Plate 33

Plate 16. Making landfalls off the Tyne, Humber, Elbe, Scheldt, Seine and Somme. . . . A Sprits'l barge, believed to be *Lord Warden*, and a boomie, possibly *Davenport* in the Seine. (Picture by Courtesy of the Late Captain Jack Spitty).

Plate 17. A stack barge of the 1880's, the Howard built, *Rose*, seen carrying a low stack in London River. (Picture by Courtesy of the Executors of the Late E. P. Olney).

shows three colliers at Whittle's Faversham Wharf sometime in the 1890's—yet it was accepted that these craft had their limitations, not least among them the large crew required for handling, and their deep drafts which encumbered passage up the smaller waterways on all but the very highest tides. Anxious then to evolve a still larger hermaphrodite craft which would combine the qualities of a schooner with the advantages of a barge, to be capable of working the coal trade to the shallow estuary creeks, some owners began in the 1860's to experiment with schooner rigged barge hulls. The result was the schooner and barquentine barge.

Two noted Milton schooner barges, owned at Burnham by John Smith, were *Friendship*, and *Emily Lloyd* of 126 tons, and one of the last of this ilk to be built was the Murston barquentine barge *S.D.* Absolutely dwarfing the sprits'l barges in Faversham Creek where she was owned, Plate 34 shows her being nosed into her berth by the paddle tug *Pioneer*. Of 131 tons *S.D.* measured 97 feet by 23.4 feet by 8.1 feet. Her Master was a Faversham man, Captain Duncan and William Bunting recalls that his brother was seaman, then Mate in her. The barge often brought granite plinths from Cherbourg, and brought stone from Portland for the base of part of London County Hall. She also made a number of voyages to Scotland, and it was in October 1902 while bound from Sittingbourne to Grangemouth that she struck Inchgarvie, and was towed to Port Edgar where she sank. Raised, it was only nine months later that she was in collision, barley laden, while on her way to Southampton. Her end came when she was sunk by a German submarine in the Great War. Surprisingly, as they were weakly built for their size, some of these leviathans lasted to a respectable age, and the *Emily Smeed* was afloat under jury rig at Lowestoft some 60 years after building.

A traditional home of big barges was Whitstable, where Gann and The Whitstable Shipping Company also owned a number of smaller barges, like the Hollow Shore built *Why Not*, as well as a fleet of brigantines and barquentines. Of the latter *Lena*, *Ibis*, *Brenda* and *Sela*, whose hulk lies on the beach at Neyland, were all built at Prince Edward Island. Perhaps I might allow my pen to wander here and explain that there were no regular shipwrights on Prince Edward Island, but it was a traditional source of soft-wood timber, to which British owners would sail out a crew, with shipwrights, who would cut the timber to build a craft, and on completion sail it back across the Atlantic.

Now, towards the end of the 19th century, the sprits'l barge was reaching perfection in design. Over the span of a century the hull and rigging had been constantly improved; wire rigging replaced hemp cordage, iron blocks with patent sheaves became used instead of the heavy, wood ones, headsticks were fitted to the tops'ls which were no longer loose and flat-headed, and with the introduction of the wheel mizzen masts came inboard. At Harwich, Ipswich and at Littlehampton on the Sussex coast ketch barges were still being built, but for North Sea and Channel work there was to be a further adaptation of the sprits'l rig in the form of a sprit rigged mainmast and a standing gaff mizzen: craft of this rig were known as "mulies". Mike Hicks' photograph, (Plate 35) shows the "mulie" *Cambria* on one of her last trading passages under sail in 1970, which was almost the last freight to be carried by a pure sailorman, that is without an engine, although since then the fully rigged auxiliary barge *May* has delivered a small number of freights of sugar to the Isle of Wight as part cargoes, and in 1972 brought 50 tons of Portland stone to London to be used for restoration work on St. Paul's Cathedral. Later a number of ketch barges

Plate 19. A Harwich built coaster of the 1890's . . . Cann Brother's *Centaur* taking part in one of the Medway barge matches. (Picture the Author).

Plate 20. The Kent coast tops'l rig (1) The Sittingbourne owned *Fairy* of the 1860's. She carries two shrouds either side and backstays have been removed for ease of handling the cargo. Note the massive iron-banded, wood stayfall blocks and aft the barrico on the port side of the cabin top. (Picture by Courtesy of the Executors of the Late E. P. Olney).

Plate 21. The Kent Coast tops'l rig (2), the *William Bennett*. (Picture Alan Cordell, from a painting).

were re-rigged as "mulies"; Paul's McLearon-built *Alice May* was one of these.

Of the last barges to be built many were of iron and steel. They were perhaps not all as graceful as their wooden sisters, indeed I have always considered Everard's big quartet to be astonishingly ugly. Some of them are illustrated here; Goldsmith's *Cambria*, one of the noted fleet of "ironpots", Paul's *Aidie*, and Horlock's magnificent Mistleymen of which *Portlight*, *Xylonite* and *Repertor* were among the last trading barges to keep their sails. Alas not all barges were as attractive to look at as the Mistleymen. *Aidie* was one of two steel barge hulls built at Brightlingsea where so many famous barges had been launched, but these were poor looking ships. Plate 37 shows their enormous, graceless design.

H. Warrington Smyth in his "Mast and Sail in Europe and Asia" described the sprits'l barges as "without exception the handiest carriers in the world"; and the word "ubiquitous" has been used in print many times to depict that sea-going quality which enabled them to go almost anywhere around our coasts. They became the largest fleet in Europe . . . soon they were to become the only remaining fleet under sail.

Briefly, these were just some among a great variety of craft which contributed to the history of the sprits'l barge: nearly 180 of them remain today, privately owned, owned by companies, which are yachts, motor barge yachts, or are craft which have come out of trade and are under restoration; the greatest number are housebarges. Their average age, I calculate, is 71 and from the index it will be seen that a number of them were built before the century began.

Barges were built up until 1930. By then, however, the usefulness of sail as a total means of propulsion was limited, so when *Olive May*, composite built on steel frames and the largest wooden barge, was launched in 1920 she was fitted with an auxiliary engine. Then owners anxiously facing competition from the motor ship and motor lorry began to convert many of their barges to auxiliary power. Those which were fitted with engines before the last war were to predict the pattern by which those few years of post-war trade were to be conducted.

Plate 22. The remains of one of the earliest barges, the chalk barge *Admiral Blake* (Picture the Author).

Chapter II
BARGE PORTS AND TRADING DAYS

By the middle of the 18th century, almost every town on the East Coast situated by any creek or river to which access could possibly be gained was concerning itself with water-borne transport. Villages suddenly grew to enjoy brief prosperity. Today you will find remains of enlarged outfalls or docks such as those on the Swale or Dengie Hundred, far from any form of habitation, where as many as half a dozen barges used to lie alongside together. Some of these could not strictly be called barge ports as they were flourishing long before the sailing barge evolved, but later on, when the barks and cutters had disappeared, Colchester, Maldon and Faversham came to be remembered for their sprits'l barges. Some ports grew suddenly and swiftly to meet a specific demand, like Lower Halstow which came to be of importance in the 1870's with the arrival of the brick barges. But later with the demise of traffic, its wharves fell into disuse until only the remains of the craft lying outside the creek and the occasional barge yacht who makes her home near the church reminds one of Eastwood's fleet which sailed out of here and when the population of the village rose to 700 persons. No trading ships now come to Conyer; to Goldhanger where there were once two-storey maltings and where rocksalt was unloaded; or to Beaumont where in the 1830's a cut was dug and a quay built, said to have been constructed from stones of the old London Bridge, demolished in the 1830's.

Barge wharves were constructed as and when they were required. A favourite method of building them was to sink a barge across the marshes and fill it in as the base of the wharf. Smeed Dean's berths were constructed in this way, *Monitor* and *Florence* being built in to the top and bottom of Marsh Berth. The centre of the wharf was piled. Both barges had previously sunk, *Monitor* hitting Kew Bridge and killing her Mate, *Florence* sinking off Tilbury Fort. Daniel's former *Azima* was used for wharfing at Strood, and when Tom Redshaw went down to Otterham once after there had been considerable erosion of the bank he found the wharf had been built up on old barge hulls. There was a whole line of them, round-bowed, all stripped off to deck level.

How then did these towns and villages about which we write become ports? Water transport on this coast was known at least in Roman times when corn and pottery were carried to the principal towns and sometimes overseas. The coastline has changed much since those times; towns like Rye, Appledore and New Romney

Plate 23. The cutter-rigged hoy barge *Good Intent* pictured at Whitstable over a century ago. Like many of the earlier 19th century hoys she was double-ended and described as being of "smack-rig". (Picture Conway Picture Library).

Plate 24. The first true sprits'l barges, albeit without mizzen masts, used in the chalk, lime and stack trades. Note the raised cabin top and obviously crudely built after-cabin. From an engraving by W. H. Pyne, (Peter Smith, Luton Museum and Art Gallery).

were once on the Rother Estuary when Dungeness was an island and old Winchelsea lay to the east and not to the west of Rye as now; Thanet was an Island and the Wantsum up to Reculver was a wide channel. Ships sailed through here to inside the Isle of Sheppey, which at its narrowest was half a mile wide, Harty being a complete island. Where Stangate and Half Acre Creeks are now there was dry land with no marshland creeks, the half-tidal islands of Burntwick and Milford Hope were then Roman pottery centres. Further down the coast along the present border of Norfolk and Suffolk was the great estuary of Garienisostium, as wide as Breydon Water is now long.

From these times right up until a century and a quarter ago there had been only two methods by which cargo could be moved from one place to another, by cart or by water. The former was slower, more costly and came to be dangerous. Even as late as 1800, carts were advertised as "proceeding in caravans for safety .." for South East Essex and North Kent were lawless places where, according to C. Edgar Thomas: "the inhabitants were notorious for their rebellious spirit, their uncouth and almost uncivilized manner of being and their amazing drinking capabilities . . ."

Medieval East Anglian life rotated on three principal activities: fishing, farming and the manufacture of cloth. It was cloth which generated such a powerful wealth until fleeces became the most valuable commodity in the North Sea and they were even smuggled out of this country. And with this wealth magnificent merchant centres and beautiful churches were built. Some of the stone for these came from France via the port of Maldon. There are records that in 1420 one Thomas Westcote hired a cart from the Abbot of Beeleigh, at 2/6d. for a week, to carry stone from Maldon to Chelmsford; and that in 1500 harbour dues of 10d. were collected at the port from a ship of Normandy laden with "cane-stonys", possibly destined for St. Mary's at Chelmsford which was to be re-edified shortly afterwards.

From around 1600 corn and other valuable commodities borne on the coast were entrusted to vessels which became known as the hoys. These formed a reliable and regular means of communication and on their trade was built the subsequent fortunes of the sailing barge. Hoy barges were certainly known at Maldon in 1623, for in that year when the bailiffs, Thomas Hutt and Jeremy Pratt, issued a warrant to the constables requiring them to make enquiry of the craft, their burdens and ordnance, together with a notice of all seafaring men, it was found that five hoys were owned in the town. They were *Dyamund*, *Marie & John*, *Fortune*, *Thomas*, and the *Blessing* which at 54 tons was the largest. Some of these obviously worked the coal trade for the enquiry found that two of the seafarers, Philip Eures and Edward Hare were going to Newcastle, while a third, Edward Lee, was "at Newcastle".

Regular hoy sailings came to be advertised. Lowndes' Directory for 1773 records that Maldon hoys sailed from Brown's Wharf at St. Catherine's, those from Faversham sailed from Wool Quay near Custom House, while Snape and Woodbridge hoys sailed from near-by Dice Quay. It was now common for village ports to have

their own quays to serve the newly built granaries, maltings and lime kilns. At Milton Regis, Heybridge Village, Mersea Strood, Stambridge and Woodbridge there were tide mills, while other landings had windmills, where millers like John Crozier at Beeleigh Abbey owned their own corn sloops. Other ports developed later. At Battlesbridge for example the maltings and kilns were not built until after 1769 when the old Hull Bridge fell down, and although a new one was built at County expense, presumably access was granted up river for a tide mill was then built. When the Chelmer and Blackwater Navigation was built following the embittered fight by the Maldoners who feared loss of custom and dues—the fight lasted for 62 years—the little villages along the canal route suddenly became open to trade. The prestige of the canal was enormous, the miller at Woodham Walter's Blue Mill proudly announcing that his mill was now convenient for the canal. Until then chalk, coal and stone were being transported by cart at around 1/-. per mile per one-and-a-quarter ton cartloads, hauled by teams of five horses and two men. Yet a shipowner could purchase chalk at Gravesend for only 2/6d. per cartload, discharging it at Maldon Quay for 10/-. A freight rate of 7/6d., which was only 6d. less than the cart charge to Chelmsford, while to Dunmow the charge was 15/-.

Trade to and from the Kent and Essex ports was mainly agricultural. Cereals, root crops and hay were the outward cargoes with return freights of muck, lime, stone and chalk. The indication of the amount of coastal sea traffic is evidenced by one port,

Plate 27. Stumpy barges of the 1860's. The well known *Mars*, 33 tons, built in 1868 and winner of the Thames Match of 1871. These craft were bowsprit rigged for racing, and their masts often raked slightly aft. (Picture M. A. Farnham Collection).

Faversham, which in the 1790's owned 6 colliers, 13 larger vessels in the Baltic trade, 100 smacks, a number of smaller sloops and corn barges, and four hoys, a total of probably around 2,000 tons of sail.

The hoys, *Rochford*, *Kent*, *Phoenix* and *Adventure* which were sailed by Captains Nixon, Holmes, Underdown, and Jones respectively, took goods and cleared London every Tuesday. The actual hoymen were James and Henry Jones, and Ed. Fairbrass. One, William Wilson was appointed to the quaintly-termed office of Clerk to the Hoys. The first three of this quartet were to lead long sailing lives, and *Kent* which at 88 tons was described as smack rigged survived for nearly a century. In 1867 and 1875 *Phoenix* and *Kent* respectively were replaced by new sprits'l rigged barges carrying their old names.

At Maldon in the same period the hoys were owned by the Sadd and Drake families, taking goods from Harrison's Wharf "but not regularly on account of the moon as they endeavour to get here (to Maldon) near the new and full moon on account of the tide. These vessels which take in goods are called packets, and most frequently take in on Fridays and Saturdays.... " Not a very helpful description. Not all the hoys traded from London for at Colchester two of them ran regularly to Hull and Gainsborough. Some of their names were undoubtedly chosen to signify solidity and reliability: *Olive Branch*, *Constant Trader* and *Resolution*; although Walsh's Salcott owned hoy was named *Robin Hood*! It was perhaps two merchants of new found fortune who were later inspired to name their craft *Friends Increase* and *New Prosperous*.

The rise in fortunes of these East Coast ports early in the 19th century was phenomenal. At its commencement Maldon boasted 9 merchant shippers, 3 hoymen and 6 shipwrights, yet a half-century later the port was seeing 2,500 ship movements a year bringing 57,680 tons of coal, 45,569 quarters of wheat and the same of flour. The railway had come to Maldon, planned to become a great East Coast terminus, and a dock was dug behind the station. Brigs and schooners sailed under the flags of Sadd, Smee, and Tovee; Joseph Ward converted Beeleigh Abbey mill to steam power; there were timber yards, sail lofts, rope mills, ironworks and bonded warehouses. But the Railway Company expected too much from the age of steam: the great dock was never used and Maldon became the Port that "Never Was."

All this is history. But it was on this foundation that the sprit-rigged barge emerged from the Estuary into North East Kent and down the Essex coast in the early years of the 19th century, taking over trades which had been the prerogative of the sloops, the cutters and the billy boy ketches, ousting them from the corn and building materials trades. And when it became evident that the East Coast towns would never become the great railway termini envisaged by some, shippers began to concentrate again on short passage trades for which the sprits'l barge was to prove such an ideal medium.

Plate 28. The round-bowed stumpy barge *Alfred*, which dated from the late 1840's. Note the raked bow, high-peaked sprit and aft-raking mast. Compare this with Fox Talbot's photograph which shows the mast to be for'ard raking. (Picture by Courtesy of the Executors of the Late E. P. Olney).

Trade had been the whole foundation on which Georgian England was built. The conveyance of goods was to people the most single important factor in a nation's capacity to conduct business. London cried out for bricks, tiles, cereals and rootcrops, a pattern which was to continue throughout the Victorian age.

The barge's lowness of side made her very suitable for loading on to a beach or landing. Goods could easily be run up a ramp, or at low water carts could come right up alongside and unload direct, which made the barge so ideal for work in the hay, straw and brick trades. The illustration of Fred Pryor's *Britannia* unloading bricks at Putney in the 1890's demonstrates how goods

Plate 29. Stumpy barges at Putney. (L) the Faversham owned *Harmony* of 1857, the second of that name to be owned at that port, (C) the then newly built *Annie & Alice*, and (R) the *Lizzie*, a tops'l barge. Topmasts were struck while working above bridges. (Picture by Courtesy of the Executors of the Late E. P. Olney).

were unloaded into carts. The photograph of *Constance* at Eastwood's Wharf in Milton Regis, taken around 1900, shows how shallow the creek-side berths were, while looking at the photograph of the barge straw-laden at Benfleet Ferry it is easy to wonder how on earth she ever floated and sailed away!

One of the more interesting sides to barge history is the connection with the industries whose products the barge carried afloat. It is perhaps worth describing some of them.

The traditional East Coast freight was agricultural produces. Until shortly after the Great War stack barges were a common sight loading hay and straw at farm landings and discharging them at Greenwich, East Smithfield, Vauxhall and Lambeth. On the Blackwater, one of the centres of this trade, stacks were loaded at Maldon, at Goldhanger Creek, where they came from as far away as Tiptree, at Thirslet, Mayland, Mundon, and at Salcott where William Markham had once owned the old swim-header *City of London*. At Maldon James Keeble and William Strutt were the principal merchants buying stacks as they lay in the fields all over the Hundreds. Cutting, pressing, loading and carrying was such a high art and the Maldoners were so proud of their reputation that nothing was left to chance.

Old Will Strutt used to set off to inspect each stack personally. Mrs Huffle remembers that her father used to accompany him on these inspections to make sample trusses. The cutter worked on the stack preparing trusses of 56 lbs in weight, his mate then put them onto the press while the pressers checked the weight, compressed and bound each truss, which was then tested with a hay auger. My own grandfather was a valuer, although not in Essex, and was

Plate 30. The high peaked rig of the Harwich built coaster *Freston Tower*, built by Cann in 1889. (Picture M. A. Farnham Collection).

Plate 31. A stumpy barge of the 1860's, *Rosa*. The mizzen mast is mounted to the port side of the rudder head. Note the ornately carved tiller bar, and the rather curiously banded leeboards. The top of the water barrico can be seen above the port quarter board. (Picture by Courtesy of the Executors of the Late E. P. Olney).

testing hay one day with another valuer. The chap inserted his auger, twisted the handle and it broke. Grandad turned to my father "Lend him mine, son."

"Huh!" replied Father. "It was your auger he broke."

Complete stacks were built alongside the presses and offered for sale. They were then dismantled and taken by cart to the nearest creek landing where the trusses would be loaded aboard to be rebuilt into a stack either side of the mast, laid across the deck from rail to rail each married into the next. The whole stack leaned inboard and was wedged so tight that the crew sometimes had trouble cutting passage through in order to lower the mast when coming up to London's bridges.

From memory the Hales, Vince, Eve families and the Deadman brothers were cutters at Maldon and some of the barges which carried the stacks afloat were Strutt's *James, Elizabeth & Mary, Fanny, Surprise, Two Friends, Unity, William & Arthur, Hannah;* Alf Warren's *The Sisters;* Alfred Lucking's elderly *James;* Keeble's *Thomas & Ann, Burnham, Keeble, Mundon, Eva Annie, Emily, Sunbeam, Percy,* and the *George Cookson* which was managed for Cookson of Isleworth. Other stack barges on the Blackwater

Plate 32. a & b. (Ketch or booms'l rigged barges.
(a) On the blocks at Maldon. Note the gaff-rigged main and mizzen sails, and the size of the hull in comparison with the smaller barge hull alongside. (Picture. The Author's "Dustbin Collection").

(b) The *Alexandra*, one of the few barges to be built at Poole, at Newtown, Isle of Wight. (Picture the Late Geoffrey Archdale, who crewed the barge on a number of occasions in the 1930's. By Courtesy of Mrs Barbara Tristrim).

were those of Gutteridge, William Charles Murrell (who was known as the 'Millionaire Dustman'), Matthams and John Parker. The Keebles became one of Maldon's best known bargeing families and it was James's father Thomas who had come to the town from Hullbridge where he had been born around 1800.

Among the hay and straw merchants around the coast were Woods of London, who were also barge owners at Milton, Noakes & Son of Greenwich and W. H. Wolsey of Nine Elms Lane who was one of the largest of the London dealers, purchasing hay and straw for the carriage horse and omnibus stables. After unloading in London the barges usually returned with straw muck-outs for laying on the land. It was the Rankins at Stambridge who once had a contract with the London Omnibus Company to take away manure at only 10/- per barge load! W. C. Murrell, who made his fortune from rubbish, owned tips in Milton Creek, where his wharf was opposite Shrubsall's yard. His Maldon based craft like *Esther* which were managed by his son Robert made a triangular passage, hay to London, rubbish to Milton and returned to Maldon with flints or rag stone.

Plate 33. Three colliers at Whittle's Faversham Wharf in the mid 1890's. (Picture by Courtesy of John Cotton).

Flints were also taken in great numbers to Foulness Island to keep up the sea-wall. They were unloaded on the old Broomway track, where stacks from Henry Mattham's farms at New Wick, Tree Farm and Courtsend were loaded. One of these barges was the *Emma Mizzen* of which Ike Ducker was once Master. Just after the Great War when this barge was owned by Goldfinch at Whitstable she sank, stack-laden, off Orford Bar while on passage to Faversham. Once before in 1905 she had sunk with stone near the Ovens Buoy.

In the 1870's, the Agricultural Depression settled over East Anglia. The National Agricultural Union had been formed, result-

ing from Joseph Arch's "Revolt", and in the 1880's thousands upon thousands of the nation's best farm workers emigrated. Acres were turned over to corn and grass, machinery became more widely used and suddenly the whole pattern of East Anglian agriculture changed. Possibly the bargemen benefited from this in the short term for there was plenty of work in the hay and cereals trades for them. There were mills and maltings at most ports where the operators owned their own barges. Some were readily accessible but others were awkwardly sited. For example, to reach Beccles on the Waveney a number of bridges and narrow waterways had to be negotiated; there were mills above bridges on the Stour, Colne, Chelmer and Medway; at Fingringhoe barges lay bow on and at Saltcote they went in stern-first. Billy Hamilton can remember doing this in *Edith May* before traffic to Saltcote ceased in the 1950's. At both Beaumont and at Heybridge village it was a tight squeeze. The photograph of *Gold Belt* up in the creek at Heybridge which has now been dammed was taken during the last war.

The dry-cargo trade required barges to be well-found, for grain may swell if wet and can burst a barge's seams. It was the Maidstone-owned *Ruth* which filled and sank one night, drowning her crew. She was later raised, repaired and repainted. A new Skipper was appointed and he told me that during his first freight which was sand the barge never made a drop of water. The second freight was different. He loaded grain and the barge soon began to leak, wetting part of her cargo. The Skipper quietly refused to take her away again fearing that *Ruth* might burst a seam grain-laden and sink.

The largest category of freights to be carried by the sprits'l barge was those in the building materials industry. And there was a time when during the building of Victorian, suburban London innumerable freights of bricks and cement left the Swale, Medway and North-West Kent ports on every tide. From these industries, communities like Halling, Rainham, Lower Halstow and Murston grew up.

Bricks were manufactured by a process where locally dug brick earth was mixed with mud and ashes which had come from London by barge. Mud was loaded in the Swale and Medway creeks by gangs of "muddies" using wooden fly tools. Plate 52 shows a group of them at Stoke Saltings. The mixture was then ground in a pug mill, then moulded into bricks to be dried and burnt in either kilns or clamps. I might explain here that a kiln is a series of chambers each holding around 40,000 bricks and in a continuous kiln the fire passes round from chamber to chamber, while a clamp was a single unit where clay bricks were laid in piles on floors of old bricks with brushwood in between, the whole being covered over, fired and allowed to cool. Clamps contained large quantities of bricks up to one million.

The process whereby cement is made involves the mixing of crushed chalk with liquified clay. Finely ground, this mixture is known as slurry, which at high temperature is converted into clinker and then re-ground as powder. Cement mills were sited near the chalk hills around Gravesend, Purfleet in Essex, the Upper Medway, at Conyer, on the Isle of Sheppey, and at Faversham where one product made was Roman cement, which like hydraulic lime has the property of setting under water. Lime was produced from limestone or chalk, kiln burnt and made into mortar. At one time lime mortars mixed with sand were extensively used for bedding and jointing brickwork and for plastering.

Some brickmakers also manufactured cement, while as its name suggests the Burham Brick, Lime and Cement Company made all three products. It was at their Burham works that the remains of a Mithraic Temple was found near one of the lime kilns.

The barges which were built to carry these products afloat were some of the smallest on the tideway, certain of them being required to work up through Regent's Canal, and at Burham only small barges were at one time able to reach the wharf until the new Cut was dug. The larger barges in the Eastwood fleet, *Trotter*, *Bedford* and *Mid Kent*, could load around 45,000 bricks, but the smaller stumpies took only around 30,000. Bricks were loaded from wharves and sea-walls close to the kilns and clamps, five at a time being chucked from man to man to be stowed. Cement was loaded in barrels, more recently in bags.

Plate 36. The former boomie barge *Alice May* after being converted to sprits'l rig. She carries high, light painted bow boards for'ard and appears to have been fitted out for a yachting cruise. She became a motor barge and is now a privately owned motor barge yacht. (Picture Beken of Cowes Ltd., by Courtesy of Walter F. Dowsett).

Plate 37. Steel coasting barges. The ungainly hull of *Aidie*. The device in her tops'l represents her owners "Windmill" trade brand. The barge was lost at Dunkirk. (Picture Mary Love).

Plate 38. Everard's powerful *Greenhithe*. (Picture M. A. Farnham Collection).

There were few ports which had facilities for handling cargo so that most jobs were done by hand. At Dan's Gunpowder Dock on the Swale marshes flints for roadmaking were brought in carts up to the sea-wall where they were shot down into the holds along ramps. Flints came from chalk overburdens callowed off when the brick earth was dug.

Other building materials to be carried by barge included stone, brick tiles and pipes, sand, timber and occasionally slate, which was at times brought from the Welsh quarries by boomie barges. Building sand was quarry dug but sand for the brick moulds came from dredgers in the river mouths or was loaded by the crews themselves off the foreshores. Plate 56 shows the crew of Smeed Dean's *Jessie* loading by means of fly tools. The marks of the tools can be seen in the foreground. Plate 57 shows *Esther* loading moulding sand at Lower Upnor for Ford's of Dagenham.

Timber freights comprised logs for the saw-mills, railway sleepers, fencing, and Baltic deals which were loaded mainly in the Surrey Docks. *Lady Helen, Varuna, Alaric* and the motor barge *Northdown* are seen in Plate 61 waiting to unload timber at Sadd's Maldon wharf in around 1956. The traditional way of loading and unloading timber was to bounce it up a plank, with up to a hundredweight at a time being balanced on the shoulder Plate 58a.

In the Estuary the carriage of explosives was a very specialised trade. Gunpowder was made at Waltham Abbey, on Cliffe Marshes and around Faversham, but gradually the Swale and Cliffe works were brought under the management of Curtis & Harvey. To the powder mills barges brought the ingredients of sulphur, saltpetre and charcoal which were ground into powder. But when the firm became a part of ICI and the factory was moved to Ardeer in

Plate 39. That sea-going quality which enabled a barge to go almost anywhere around our coasts . . . the *Beatrice Maud*, built at Crown Quay in 1910. (Picture M. A. Farnham Collection).

Scotland many of the old Faversham powder barges went to Denton near Gravesend eventually to be broken-up. There, near Denton, the ammunition ship from Scotland would unload into the powdermen, 25 tons at a time; the barges then lay at anchor until ships arrived to relieve them of their cargoes. Traditionally powder barges anchored in Holehaven Creek but later their moorings were removed to the Lower Hope.

But such trades were mainly confined to the Estuary and the barge was by no means a short passage trader. Coal for the various gas works was an important commodity. Although originally in

Plate 40. Maldon Hythe before the Great War, with the Howard built *Sunbeam* embarking the Mayor and Corporation for their annual inspection of the river. (Picture, the Author's "Dustbin Collection").

Plate 41. A barge, probably the *Edward*, at Iron Wharf, Faversham. The Wharf lies some distance below the town, between Standard Quay and Chambers Dock, on the new section of waterway which was dug by hand in the 1830's to avoid the wide sweep round Ham Marshes. (Picture by Courtesy of John Cotton).

the hands of collier brigs, then fore-and-afters and boomies even some of the smaller barges went off to the Tyne and the Humber. Once William Smee's round-bowed Maldoners brought coal from Sunderland to the Blackwater, and before the Great War Samuel West's Gravesend owned *Charles Allison*, later renamed *Gywnronald*, and *Lady Gwynfred* were bringing coal to Maldon from the Humber. The local lads scrambled among themselves for the job of leading the trace horse back down North Hill to earn their 6d. per day. At only 48 tons *Edith* carried Humber coal to Bruges. Under Charlie Ward *Edith* often sailed to

Plate 42. Timber laden barges at Faversham in the 1920's. Centre *James & Ann*, right stern of the schooner barge *Goldfinch*. (Picture by Courtesy of John Cotton).

Plate 43. Hoy barge sailings advertised in the Universal British Directory, 1798. (From a volume in the possession of the Bishopsgate Institute).

Plate 44. The Howard built *Ethel Maud* at the Maldon mills, hard by the bridge. (Picture Patricia O'Driscoll).

Plate 45. Cart horses and sprits'l barges. Fred Pryor's *Britannia*, built by Goldfinch (R) and the *Lady Flora* (L), in the 1880's. (Picture by Courtesy of the Executors of the Late E. P. Olney).

the Continent: once coming home from St Valery she was damaged in collision but was able to make Ramsgate safely.

When coal was brought to the East Anglian ports by Sunderland and Newcastle brigs or schooners local merchants eventually acquired their own colliers. David Garrod remembered bringing coal for the Chelmsford gas works to Heybridge Basin in the locally owned brigantine *Robert Adamson*. These colliers were sometimes leaky craft, carrying a crew of between four and five men who were paid the same money whether the voyage lasted a fortnight or a month. As the Master had to pay the crew's food he was out of pocket if there was any delay. Coal here was "jumped out" by men hanging onto the tails of a fall and jumping off a plank together to raise the coal baskets aloft. In this way 24 tons could be discharged in an hour and a half. David told Patricia O'Driscoll that for the return journey ballast was loaded off Nass Spit and was put aboard in this manner: "amidships in the main hold was a removable section of hull planking which formed a

Plate 46. *Constance* at Eastwood's Wharf, Milton Regis, around 1900, when the barge was owned by Edward Watson. (Picture Alan Cordell Collection).

Plate 47. A stack barge waiting for the tide at Benfleet Ferry. Landings such as this were important loading berths in the days when goods were loaded from carts. (Picture Walter F. Dowsett Collection).

square opening. Staging was rigged below this and crewmen threw the ballast up onto the stage while others of their number shot it into the hold. Later the planking was replaced, the edges caulked".

In addition to *Robert Adamson* the ketch barges *Pioneer*, *Emily* and the ketch *Elizabeth* worked in the Heybridge coal trade towards the end of the last century. Later David was to ship aboard the Mistley boomie *Genesta* under Harry Strange. In the summer months they carried stone to the Basin from Antwerp.

There is no space here to record more than a few of the many cargoes which the sprits'l barge carried afloat, or even to mention more than a small number of the craft themselves and their owners,

but the reader will doubtless be familiar with the works of Carr, Cooper, March and Benham in which he will find many of these answers. But I hope these paragraphs have given some percept behind trade on the East Anglian coast.

Because of the many complexities which governed the cycle of trade a Master had to be prepared to take his barge almost any-where, and this required him to have a good knowledge of the various ports.

The entrances to rivers like the Ore and Deben could change after every gale and it took a skilled man to find his way over a surf-studded bar. At Great Yarmouth where Bessie & Palmer used to own collier schooner barges like *Enterprise*, barges were regular traders, towed into the haven by the paddle tug *United Service*. Faversham, too, had a paddle tug, the *Pioneer* (Plate 34). Her successor *Noni* is seen in Plate 65 towing six sailormen up past Iron Wharf. But at most creeks no assistance other than the service of a huffler was available and in narrow waters if a barge came head to wind her crew usually had to lower the gear and trace up. Kentish men were quite used to lowering away, shooting a bridge, heaving up and sailing onto the next bridge where the procedure was repeated.

Both inshore and on coastal passages barges were caught out and sometimes sank through misfortunes. Joe Hines has kept a record of many of these instances which serve to illustrate just how far afield the barge did travel. *Centaur*, for example was in difficulty in two successive years when owned by Rogers of Chichester. In January 1905 while on passage to Exeter with sugar she lost her sprit and had to be towed into Portland for the sum of fifteen pounds. The following year trading between Rochester and Antwerp she lost both anchors off Teneuzen. They voyaged up and down the North Sea, "down Channel", and even round into the Irish Sea. Walter Dowsett acquired a photograph which shows a barge ashore in Milford Haven!

For better or for worse these days have gone and with them men have almost forgotten the harshness which sometimes made up their lives. Times like the depression, when freight rates fell so low that meal paid only 6d. per ton and maize and barley just 1/6d. per quarter, and when it was a fortunate Skipper who picked up a freight of London rubbish for the brickfields.

Plate 51. Cement barges. Byford's *Annie Byford* **(L),** *Alice Laws,* **which later sank cement laden, and (R)** *John Byford* **at the Bow Creek Depot in 1919. (Picture Alan Cordell Collection).**

Plate 52. Mud was dug from the Swale and Medway creeks and taken to the local fields for the manufacture of bricks. Here the "muddies", as they were known, are seen against the background of two barges waiting to load at Stoke. The men are holding smaller versions of the "sandie's" fly-tools, which were used for throwing the mud up and over a barge's side. The picture was taken in the 1920's. (Picture Alan Cordell Collection).

Chapter III
SAILORMEN

I have never subscribed to the popular belief that men who went to sea were of any particular breed, type or character. That they came to be stamped with certain qualities I believe was only as a result of lifetimes spent on the water, and it was this which has given them their skill, expertise and quiet understanding of life. The sailorman, the name by which bargemen were known, had much in common with the countryman restricted to the confines of his parish. Both were in a way classless societies bound up in a strong element of inevitability, for however much techniques altered, the land and the sea were always the same. Boys followed their fathers, uncles, and brothers afloat in the same way that others joined their families in the yard, field, mill or workshop because there was no alternative except that of making the definite break. They considered their tasks to be ordinary, and if perhaps they worked long hours for rewards that would be unsatisfactory to our present working man, it was because they preferred to accept this inevitability.

The sailorman was naturally a quiet and reticent man who rightly considered his life to be private. He shared a cabin in close confinement with his crew, going off to London to deliver a freight, and returning not many days later. A commuter of the tideway. When he retired it was natural for him to retain a keen interest in the sea and its happenings, meeting as retired sailormen do in Sittingbourne from time to time to discuss the old days, about ships and men they had known. Always they are prepared to give advice and assistance. In compiling this book I have sought the advice of some of these men, a number of whom first went to sea before the turn of the century and carried on working until they reached their late 60's or 70's. It is their lives, their knowledge and their experiences which have clothed these pages, but because their lives are private I have retold their experiences as they were told to me, discussing with them afterwards what I have written.

As with rural life women played an important part in this cycle afloat. It was a family existence, a bargeman's wife often coming from a bargeing family herself, and up until the Great War it was not uncommon for a Kentish barge wife to sail as mate to her husband. Plate 122 of *Our Boys* shows the master's wife standing aft, presumably about to hang the washing out. One of these ladies was Mrs Ada Fletcher who recently, at the age of 92, stepped aboard *May* berthed at Crown Quay. Mrs Fletcher was at one

"Sailorman" by the Late Peter Fraser. (By Courtesy of Rod Fraser).

time mate to her husband George "Doggy" Fletcher, master of the *Baltic*. "Doggy" began his life afloat around 1890, and retired to take a position as huffler at Kingsferry in 1933. *Baltic* was another barge which voyaged far afield, going even as far as Cornwall, and on one trip there she was wrecked at Mousehole. Three years after this incident, in 1910, we find *Baltic* on passage to Yarmouth, with the lifeboat coming out to render her assistance.

In addition to their duties as mates these ladies also managed to bring up families and provide them with a home aboard. Mrs Josephine Blake sailed as mate to her husband Sidney "Tubby" Blake in Murrell's *J.S.H.*, *Hope*, Parker's *Champion*, Wakeley's *Southwark* and *Fanny*. Their two sons, Bill and George, were brought up on board, and then when Bill was old enough he became mate of *Fanny* with his father. "Tubby" had a rare sense of humour, and of justice. As a boy aboard *Champion* Bill came back one day reporting that he had fought and lost a fight with another lad. Restitution, thought Bill, but no: "Tubby" cornered the other lad. "Did you just beat my boy in a fight?" "Tubby" enquired; and he turned to Bill "Right, it's your turn to beat him, and if you lose I'll give you a thrashing." Bill won and "Tubby" presented the contestants with sixpence each.

Captain Lissenden was master of the Faversham-owned *Why Not* when she was sold to Daniels around 1890. She was only a little barge, his son remembers, loading between 80 and 90 tons, and when he was a boy in 1900 he made a few trips with his father. Captain Lissenden was a teetotaller and a proper Chapel man. Whether in London or at home he attended the Primitive Methodist

Plate 53. The stumpy barge *Connaught* loading coal by means of a chute. (Picture M. A. Farnham Collection).

Plate 54. *Histed* loading bricks at Adelaide Dock in the 1930's. The bricks were passed five at a time from the barrow to the stower in the hold. (Picture Alan Cordell Collection).

Plate 55. The entrance to the Surrey Commercial Docks, where many of the timber freights were loaded. The barge was a small craft in comparison to the high sides of the brigs and four masted barques. (Picture M. A. Farnham Collection).

Plate 56. Loading sand aboard Smeed Dean's *Jessie* at Leigh in 1923. Left to right "Pip" Box, mate, who was later master of the APCM's last barge, the *Dunstable*, Ernie Britten, master, and right, a local "sandie". (Picture Alan Cordell Collection, by Courtesy of "Pip" Box).

Plate 56a. Loading mud in the early 1890's. Hilton, Anderson & Brooks stays'l barge *Mahatma*. Note the dodger around the wheel and the protection rigged up around the shrouds and mastcase. *Mahatma*, built in 1891, is shown here almost new from the ways. (Picture Author's Collection).

Plate 57. *Esther*, formerly owned by Cremer's, loading moulding sand at Lower Upnor. Her master, Captain Chris Merritt, is seated on the hatches. (Picture Patricia O'Driscoll).

Plate 58. Timber laden barges by Maidstone bridge just before the Great War. Note the difference in size between the two barges nearest to the camera. Maidstone was the home of Hutson's barges and a number of fine coasting barges were built for the firm here. (Picture Alan Cordell Collection).

Plate 58a. Unloading timber by hand at Sadd's Wharf, Maldon. (Picture Patricia O'Driscoll).

Church—and there were many like him.

To illustrate the sailorman's way of life I can do no better than to cite the experiences of the well-known Faversham Skipper, Captain Charles Frake, who started as a boy aboard *Oxygen* at the age of 14 and went on to become Skipper and later part owner of *Edith*. He still sometimes skippers the Thames Barge Sailing Club's barges on occasional charters and in 1972 brought Alan Reekie's *Ironsides* round from Queenborough to Crown Quay.

At the age of 75 his face is lined and full of expression, and Charlie has a quiet, unhurried way of going about business. His movements, like those of all bargemen, are slow, certain and planned in advance, allowing the barge to work for him, a perfect example of the rapport which comes to exist between a practiced master and his ship. Being a Kentishman whose lifework centred around the delivery of bricks, timber and ashes to and from the

Plate 59. Wills & Packham's *Rand* turning to wind'ard in a stiff breeze. Note the oars positioned in their rollocks and protruding over the bow. The fores'l is reefed-up to allow the helmsman for'ard vision. (Picture Arthur Bennett, by Courtesy of Alan Cordell).

Plate 60. *Ready* working a stack of timber out of London River just after the last war. (Picture C. Beazley).

Plate 61. Timber to Maldon . . . left to right Francis & Gilders *Alaric*, *Lady Helen* and *Varuna*, with the stern of the L.R.T.Co.'s *Northdown*, at Sadd's Wharf in the mid 1950's. (Photograph the Author).

shallow Swale creeks, he is under no illusions about hard work.

I watched him, sailing through the lower reaches of Faversham Creek which bends with such acuteness from Hollow Shore up to near the site of Old Thorn Quay just below the town. His hands were gently but continually playing the spokes of the wheel as one minute we were on a gybe in Skiff Reach and the next winding round Nagden Bump, perfectly stiff under main canvas, only feet away from the uncovered mud, at times needing two men at the helm to see the barge round the difficult bends. Above Nagden the barge headed-up, her bow touched and Charlie ordered the fores'l to be dropped, then seeing that she was not going to wind, the canvas was taken off her before the gear was lowered to the deck. He knew that we were lucky to reach this far. At one time we would have traced up but now there was the assistance of a small motor-boat able to help us along on the tide.

Much of Charlie's life afloat was spent with Eastwoods and then with Cremers. Of all he found *Pretoria* to be the best barge to sail, although for ease of handling he preferred *John & Mary* which had all the qualities of a lifeboat. With the brake on the wheel she would easily sail herself, but *Edith* was a bit of a terror, and could never be left unattended for long as she had weak chines and took to leaking badly.

Brick freights involved working to the up-river London wharves, where in *Iota* under skipper Alf Manuel they were towed down from Putney to Molesey Lock. Later, Charlie worked through the Regent's Canal in the little stumpy *E.F.Q.* For up-river work the gear was lowered in the "mud hole" off St. Saviour's Dock then the barge was rowed up on the tide. Coming back they would look in at the Chelsea, Vauxhall or Kennington wharves hoping to pick up a return freight of ashes.

Plate 62. An unknown tiller steered bowsprit barge with rucked topsail off the Isle of Dogs. (Popperfoto).

Plate 63. Powder barges at dusk off Denton in 1957, just before ICI's fleet of sailormen was laid up. (Picture Alan Cordell).

These little barges could crack on canvas. Passages could be fast and sometimes leaving London on the evening ebb Charlie was able to sail through the night and be off the mouth of Faversham Creek, ready for towing up on the first of the flood. But he was once caught out. When he left Wapping on one particular Wednesday night all the food he had on board was a bloater and half a loaf of bread, but being near to Christmas there was a bag of walnuts aboard, too! The barge fell fogbound and by the time they arrived off Gravesend on the Sunday night they had long since eaten everything, and the tealeaves had been boiled until they were colourless. Later, Charlie tried baking them for smokes!

A fast barge was a dirty barge and he found Eastwood's stumpies to be very dirty in a sea-way. The crews referred to them as "flat-irons", but they were well-kept down below; the cabins were smart and the Company even gave a prize for the best-kept cabin, which Charlie remembers Tom Cook in *Delta* winning one year. Even Cremer's barges could be dirty at times—although *John & Mary* was a noted exception however hard it blew, Charlie found she could always be steered and would never punish her crew. Once with Alf Manuel bringing back timber to Faversham, Charlie noticed that the stack was behaving strangely. He went up for'ard and found that every time the barge buried her head the sea was running under the stack and lifting it up. The barge was off Warden Point at the time and as the mouth of the East Swale could be a dirty place in a blow Alf ran her back into Sheerness for shelter.

It was off the mouth of the East Swale, around 1922, that Charlie encountered a waterspout. He was sailing then as mate to Alf in *John & Mary*.

In a fair breeze off Tankerton they saw behind them a white funnel, spurting up. Alf let the tops'l halyard go and was starting to get the mains'l off when a waterspout struck on the port-aft side, laying the barge over so hard that the side of her coal stack was submerged. This appeared to have broken the waterspout and the barge was able to limp back into Faversham. On arrival Lewis "Lou" Wood on the *Bertie* called out "Did you see that water-spout?"

"See it, we hit it, look at the remains of our mains'l," was the reply. But had the spout struck on the starboard side the barge would have heeled to port and the sea filled in through the cabin scuttleway.

When Charlie joined *Oxygen* as a boy his first voyage was coke to France where he later spent his 14th birthday in Calais Harbour. On a subsequent trip *Oxygen* loaded pitch to Dieppe where they were towed up the Somme to load "boulders" at St. Valery after-wards. Here they could hear the sound of the big guns firing only a few miles away. His connection with *Oxygen* was to be short, and it was not long before he was ashore.

"It was the roast" he explained regretfully. "Me and the mate had words. I put the roast in the oven with the stove low and nipped ashore for the afternoon. I came back to find the mate had returned, stoked the fire up and the roast was burnt to a cinder. Of course, I had to to leave the barge".

Plate 64. Towing out of Great Yarmouth harbour . . . the paddle tug *United Service* towing *Alf Everard* and *Will Everard* to sea. (Picture by P. A. Vicary).

Plate 65. Since the mid 19th century a tug-boat has been available to tow barges in and out of the tortuous, winding Faversham Creek. Here *Noni* tows six sailormen up past Iron Wharf. (Picture Author's Collection).

Plate 66. A tops'l barge heaving up after passing under Rochester bridges. The third man up for'ard is the huffler who was taken on to help the barge through. It was common to shoot these bridges under sail, with tops'l rucked without lowering the topmast if the barge was going on up to Aylesford, as the barges required their tops'ls in order to catch the wind above the high trees. (Picture Alan Cordell Collection).

Plate 66b. Gear on deck, the *Esther* at Colchester's Hythe Quay. Barges lowered down at the Hythe before passing under the bridges to reach East Mills. (Picture Walter F. Dowsett Collection).

It was not long before Charlie was back on the water sailing out of Gravesend in an ammunition barge, and from there he went into Eastwood's fleet, coming to Faversham in 1922. His first command was *Atlas*, in 1928. Work to the port was principally bricks, timber, ashes, coke, coal from Erith, and spent-oxide. It was hard work. "You had to row through the bridges, and you very seldom took on a 3rd Hand to help you through. You couldn't afford it then." But if brickwork was hard, sand was backbreaking. In *John & Mary* they used to sail across the Estuary for sand which would be hand loaded by the crew. When Charlie returned home after each passage he was too tired to do anything!

Charlie recalled that at the time he took *Atlas*, men were lucky to be employed. Jobs were hard to find and however bad one was you knew it might not be possible to find another one. Those that were unemployed went on public assistance. Men on the "Public" dug out the Creek or broke up stone for the sea-walls.

Charlie found the Faversham crews good men to work with and in hard times the masters would never allow their mates to go hungry. Some of the Sittingbourne bargemen, however, were a bit sharp when under-way. If you were lying off the mouth of Milton Creek you had to make sail the moment the tide flowed, otherwise if there were any of Burley's barges astern of you, they would push you out of the way to get through first. When freights were short, barges used to jostle to get alongside the rubbish wharves for a cargo home.

Sometimes the Faversham barges had to work outside the Estuary. If Charlie was not familiar with the particular creek he

Plate 67. The advent of the motor omnibus. Eastwood's Depot seen across from Southwark bridge. In the foreground is a van belonging to J. & W. Meyell. This firm is still in existence today. (Picture Author's Collection).

Plate 68. Sprits'l barges used as lifting craft during the raising of the sunken barque *Samuel* in the 1850's. The right-hand barge has a budget stern, that on the left the narrow-pointed stern which followed the budget stern into fashion. (Picture Illustrated London News).

was bound for, he tried to arrive off the mouth at low water, and sail up over the ground, on the first of the tide. *Edith* had been working to Oakley Dock in the Hamford Waters, taking up ammonia and returning with drums of acid. When her master, Charlie Ward, broke an arm Charlie Frake took the barge over for a while. The mate had been to Oakley before but it was a difficult dock to reach. Charlie's sailing directions were simple:

"Up the third creek and hard round the withies!"

I asked Percy Brown, who first went to sea before 1900, what it was like afloat in Edwardian days. "Well, we were paid two quid a month as ordinary seamen in the coasters and we earned it," was his opinion. One freight even cost Percy a pair of shoes.

Percy had shipped aboard the Littlehampton boomie barge *Lord Lansdowne*, commanded by Captain Gregory, a Faversham man. She loaded scrap horseshoes for the Tyne and in heavy weather was towed down to the Nore. Later off Robin Hood's Bay she was caught out and most of her sails were blown to pieces. The paddle tug *Ondine* (sic) came out to look for her, rolling her sponsons under in the swell. "Want a tow?" yelled the tugmaster.

"How much?"

Captain Gregory settled at two pounds, plus five shillings allow-

ance, then *Ondine* towed them up into the Northumberland.

Now the horseshoes for some reason had their nails in them which made it difficult for the freight to be unloaded, the crew having to use stone forks. "Those nails were cruel," remembered Percy bitterly. "I ruined a nearly new pair of shoes on them." Out of 10/- a week this was a serious item of expenditure.

Lord Lansdowne lay in the Tyne for nearly six weeks as there was a strike on, before finally loading coal for Essex. After that Percy paid-off and went deep water.

It had been the great-great-grandfathers of this generation of bargemen who had learned how to dodge the press gangs of George III's Navy. As I have recorded in the Journal of the Society for Spritsail Barge Research many of them were successful in this art. One Skipper, Abraham Vandervord of the *Pitsea*, actually possessed a statement sworn at Milton-next-Gravesend in June 1777, which it is believed constituted a pass for exemption from the Press Gang. Abraham was described as being 5 feet 5 inches high "of a fair complexion and wearing his own hair." The said barge was "employed in carrying of corn lime and faggots between London and Harwich only. . . ." This pass was probably obtained for him by *Pitsea's* owner, John Cousins. The East Coast sailormen

Plate 72. "Doggy" Fletcher's *Baltic* in Broadstairs Harbour in 1905. The barge was owned by Harry Keep of Lower Thames Street. (Picture Alan Cordell Collection).

Plate 73. The late Captain Frank Farrington examining the remains of *Baltic* in Milton Creek. Frank, who was formerly master of *Murston, Sam* and *Leslie* died in September 1972 (Picture Alan Cordell).

Plate 74. The late Sidney "Tubby" Blake, a man with a rare sense of humour, and of justice, pictured during the time he was master of the little barge yacht *Good Templar*, in which he once voyaged to Holland. The buttonhole was not a regular feature of "Tubby's" dress. (Picture by Courtesy of Margaret Blake).

Plate 75. The Blake family have been watermen for 300 years, coming originally from Northfleet. Here "Tubby's" eldest son, Sidney "Bill" Blake takes *Venta* round the outer mark in the 1963 Blackwater Match. (Picture the Author).

were a valuable source of manpower for the Navy, but since The Middle Ages these men had shown a marked dislike for the wars of their monarchs. In the times when the ports had to provide armed and manned ships for war duty it is frequently recorded that the Maldon ship failed to turn up for duty. So, during the Napoleonic Wars when Sea Fencible Units were raised for the defence of the coastline, the Maldoners would only board whichever ship happened to be nearest to the shore at the time; which caused Captain Schornberg at Harwich to write to Nelson that whereas there was no shortage of volunteers to man the craft ". . . it is inconceivable the difficulty I find when the time arises to persuade them to embark. . . "

Perhaps as a result of this attitude contemporary accounts began to appear which suggested that these sailormen were a brusque, hard-living bunch, whose conditions were inferior to those of the dock or agricultural worker, with a behaviour that was deplorable; fishing, fighting among themselves, working freights of chalk and manure in roughly-built craft, supplementing their incomes from any opportunity to smuggle, salvage or pilfer. Some of this is undoubtedly true and serious smuggling by the coasters continued until well within memory, yet masters held responsible positions, and it is difficult to correlate the picture some writers painted with the factual knowledge we have. Dutt certainly held the East coast sailorman in high esteem, and so apparently did Henry Mayhew, who in "London Labour and the London Poor" published in 1851 described lightermen and bargemen thus:

"They are a sober class of men, both the working masters and the men they employ. A drunken lighterman, I was told, would hardly be trusted twice." And this was probably the crux of the matter, for a sailorman's first concern was always for his ship and his cargo. Mayhew was not biased in his opinion of men connected with the water, for he describes the dock labourers as a "Striking instance of mere brute force with brute appetites."

I will say no more.

Conditions at sea, especially for the crewmen, were hard. Even a barge had few comforts, the food was poor and the risks were high. With the foresight of industrial militancy which has crept into many employments one may be tempted to ask why sailormen put up with these conditions—rough cargoes, worked seven days a week, no holidays, and no security for their families if they came to be out of work—why did they not form a union as the agricultural workers did? Well, the answer is that they did protest, and unlike the agricultural workers it probably brought them greater benefits. In 1912 there was the Dock Strike and the bargemen joined in. One or two of the older chaps are able to recall what became known as the Bargemen's Strike; when the barges were chained across Milton Creek to prevent entry or departure.

The real point of issue appears to have been freight rates, but the bargemen became generally involved with the Dock Strike. It lasted for ten weeks. Mrs Olive May Howton, daughter of Captain Arthur Wenban, was a child at the time, and the family lived at the New Inn (later the Wyf of Bath) at Milton Regis. Arthur Wenban,

Plate 76. A face so lined and full of expression—Captain Charles Frake exchanging words with the master of a Harrison liner who wanted to get out of the dock first. (Picture John Cotton).

Plate 77. Two men at the helm to see the barge round the difficult bends. Left Harry Parter the Faversham Pilot, right Charlie Frake. (Picture John Cotton).

who owned *Ethel Edith* which was trading to France at that time, the *Beatrice Maud* and the *Lord Nelson*, had a position of great influence among the bargemen. He brought about a meeting between Harry Gosling (President of the National Transport Workers Federation), Mr Lloyd (of Lloyd's Paper Mills) and, for so important was this meeting, Lloyd George the politician.

The strike was fought with great bitterness on both sides, and the workers received a considerable set-back. When the strike was over the bargemen presented Captain Wenban with a marble clock in recognition of all his efforts on their behalf.

The masters, at least before the Great War, led a superior life. Some were rewarded with small pensions on retirement, while Will Strutt had five cottages built in Maldon High Street which were tenanted to his skippers. Some owners took a great interest in both the moral and physical well-being of their employees. Those with religious principles would not allow their craft to leave port on days of worship. "But of course, that did not mean that we had the day off" one retired Faversham skipper recalled. "There was plenty of work to be done aboard. And, when I was a boy" here he grinned at this remembrance, "Why, I was taken off to church with the owner. Only I had to lend a hand to pump the organ!"

An independent life made for an irregular existence and bargemen needed some form of philosophy behind them. Several found this in their sense of humour which was ready and at the best of times very dry.

Jimmy Waldock remembers that *Golden Fleece*, which now lies as a housebarge in Ipswich River, could be very difficult to handle at times. After a particularly trying passage her Skipper "Add" Eve brought her into the Royal Albert Basin. The Pier Master came striding along and enquired of "Add" if he was the master of that barge.

Quietly removing his pipe old "Add" replied:
"Well, it's like this—sometimes I is, an' sometimes I isn't!"

Plate 78a, and b. A quiet unhurried way of going about business. (Pictures John Cotton).

Chapter IV
THE LIFE ABOARD

The very nature of his job made the bargeman a person of many parts. A master was navigator, helmsman, pilot, ship's husband, stevedore, tow-horse and extemporizer extra-ordinary. It was up-rivers, in the dockland or in confined waterways that he really came into his own to demonstrate the unique skills which made him one of the most respected men on the tideway. His life consisted of two different worlds—among the rattle and banter of London River one tide, and the next, way down the Estuary among the swatchways or marshlands.

Life aboard a barge followed an almost rigid pattern; there was only one way to do things and this was observed aboard most barges. However rough the work a barge was engaged in, her crew always attempted to keep her as smart as conditions would permit, by scrubbing and by stowing everything and lashing it down in its proper place; and in all things there was a high degree of precedent. Things were done because they had always been done, and Patricia O'Driscoll has recorded that superstition consciously or uncon-sciously played an important part in a bargeman's life. For example, a hatch was never capsized, a knife never stuck in the mast, and no self-respecting bargeman would ever consider opening a tin of condensed milk with the label upside down! The wooden knob which secured the bob frame to the spindle was carved in the shape of an acorn; this was also a protective symbol, which Patricia found reflected the old Druidic belief that as the oak was sacred to Thor, the god of thunder, that tree was never struck by lightning.

For the greater part of their lives the cabin was a crew's home, and although following a pattern in design and layout, each was imbued with a character entirely personal to the Master. Snug but never spaciously roomy, the cabin was a retreat where the Master was allowed scope to express his individuality in the high graining or varnishing of the locker doors with their brass or glass knobs, in the highly polished cabin lamps and the brass fenders above or below the cabin stove. As the cabin was tucked between the fine quarters it had to be compact, and in all except the larger barges additional height was given by means of a raised cabin top and skylight. Traditionally, the layout comprised two partly enclosed bunks, sometimes fitted with sliding doors, or oval openings, below which ran a "U" shaped sofa with lockers beneath and with a hinge flap table in the centre. In a coasting barge a Master might have his own separate stateroom. The large after-locker, panelled in pine or mahogany, was known as the "Yarmouth Roads." The floor covering was linoleum which was washed but never scrubbed to preserve the pattern.

As so much of the bargeman's life was spent in London's River either in the tideway or in the docks, it is perhaps worth recording how sailormen coped with their dual existence. Working the river could be exhausting—threading the barge in and out of passing lanes of traffic; attempting at the same time to use wind and tide to the best advantage. With a wooden hull the barge was especially vulnerable to damage either from collision or from sitting on a bad berth. There was a time when wharf owners kept their berths in pristine condition, employing men to clean the beds, but the

Plate 79. Dock work—Whitstable harbour. (Picture Douglas West Collection).

Plate 80. The important thing is ter keep yer fag alight in a blow . . . *Esther*'s *"Beefy"* **Wildish. (Picture John Cotton).**

Londoner delights in using the Thames as a rubbish tip, and has an uncanny knack of being able to dump a perambulator just before a barge arrives.

Before entering a lock, the anchor was dropped until the stock was awash, with its flukes hanging below the forefoot so they would do no damage if the barge touched. Once inside the docks a crew had to reckon on tracing the barge up to her berth, and this was done by laying out a dolly wire from the barrel above the windlass to a lighter, bollard or other fixed point while the crew wound the barge forward on the winch. Progress was slow and care had to be taken that the low sides were not trapped under the overhanging

Plate 81. Cremer's *Pretoria*, Charlie Frake found her to be the best barge to sail. She had very attractive lines and her deck view was enhanced by white capping to her bow rails. (Picture Patricia O'Driscoll).

Plate 82. Captain Ben Phillips at the chaff-cutter wheel of *Pretoria*. The barge was converted to a yacht in the early 1950's by Commander Horncastle, RN, and became a floating home for him in Germany, on the Tyne and then on the Deben, and was later sold to become briefly a floating restaurant at Pimlico. (Picture Patricia O'Driscoll).

Plate 83. "I don't know . . . but they tell me." Harold Smy of *Beatrice Maud* yarns with Barry Pearce. (Picture Patricia O'Driscoll).

Plate 84. Keeping a look-out. Right, Charles Parr, former master of the *Derby*, feet planted firmly on the deck, keeps look-out while the barge runs dart before the wind. Left, the Author crouches in order to see under the mains'l.

Plate 85. An old-time bargeman. Captain W. H. Owen was master of *Nellie Maud* and *Baden Powell*, and around the turn of the century was one of Faversham's last hoy skippers. (Picture by Courtesy of Mary Owen).

swims of the lighters, for these could easily smash the bow or quarter rails of a wooden barge, or they could be crushed by larger vessels as happened to the *Jane* in 1947. In the Royal or Surrey docks a crew had to negotiate passage through the mass of lighters which always crowded the entrances. Occasionally, but only when the barge was inexorably trapped among other craft, a P.L.A. tug would grudgingly come and offer a tow. At every turn, language, friendly or otherwise, would be exchanged with neighbouring lightermen. The lighterman was the most maligned creature in the dockland; highly trained he enjoyed a thankless task for not only did he have to control his craft without benefit of motive power he was also the butt for personal abuse from every other dock worker. But they were not men without skill for rowing a lighter is one of the high arts of the river.

For the sailormen, the most difficult docks to negotiate were the now closed down Surrey group where it was necessary to work through an intricate maze of narrow waterways to find your ship in one of the backwater yards. Bound for Russia Yard, for example, there were a number of swing bridges, and arrival somehow always coincided with the time the bridgeman was settling down to his tea—they drank a lot of tea, those chaps!

Having received orders to load in the morning the barge was taken alongside the ship ready to receive her cargo, while her crew waited for the Shipworker to appear. Patricia O'Driscoll recounts what happened when, within the last few years, dockwork changed with the introduction of the two-shift system.

"After you have traced the Shipworker, you find that he doesn't want your motor barge yet, but may do so later. So you find a berth as near to the ship as possible and give him a look about 9 a.m.—then another look, until you grow tired of the sight of each other—in the meantime you 'phone the owner's office to report progress (if any). Finally the Shipworker decides that he isn't working the barge on the morning shift, so you have to wait until 3 p.m. before trying again, to give the afternoon shift time to get themselves sorted-out. But even then you may have to hang about for another couple of hours before finding out that the barge is not required. This can go on for several days, and even if you live in London and go home for the night you have to turn-out at about 4 a.m. to be certain of being back aboard in time for the 7 a.m. start, or sure as fate they'll have landed your cargo and there's hell to pay.

"The introduction of the two-shift system into the PLA docks has proved a mixed blessing from the start. Theoretically it is a good thing, but when one moves away from theory into practice it becomes less attractive. Before 1970, working hours were from 8 a.m. until 5 p.m., with overtime until 7 p.m. Now they are from 7 a.m. until 9 p.m., the shifts changing over at 2 p.m. This suits dockworkers, lightermen, tugmen, etc., but the bargeman has the same craft all the time, unlike the lighterman, so that shifts can hardly be worked. This means that while other workers do less hours, the bargeman does more than ever, in addition to the time spent under-way.

"In spite of the fact that ships can now be worked from 7 a.m. to 9 p.m., the tonnage of the cargo handled has dropped appreciably since the dockers were put on a weekly wage. Down went the tonnage and up went the eyebrows in the office. The bargemen were not surprised.

"Nowadays the barge crews get far better overtime rates than was once the case. I can remember the time when work on a Sunday was rewarded by £1, and if one worked from 5 to 7 p.m. on a weekday one got 3/-., a weird payment known as "tea money."

"This was not forty years ago, but in the last decade, and there was often a quibble about paying both crew members.

Plate 86. A man who grew up with sailing barges. A familiar figure at Maldon Hythe, Barry Pearce has stayed with barges since he left school. (Picture the Author).

Plate 87. Captain John Fairbrother at the wheel of Cranfield's *Venture*. John was one of the last to command a barge under sail in trade, and now sails his charter barge yacht, *Kitty*, known for registration purposes as *My Kitty*. (Picture Patricia O'Driscoll).

Plate 88a, and b. Champion Racing Skippers . . . (a) A look of intense seriousness on Captain A. H. "Chubb" Horlock's face as he sails *May*. He was formerly master of *Oxygen* in trade. (Picture Alan Cordell). (b) The late Captain Jack Spitty of *Edith May*, with (right) Stanley Cook, first Hon. Treasurer of the B.S.B.M. (Picture by Courtesy of Stanley Cook).

"We took the money on principle, as we considered that it was better in our pockets, but at least one skipper I knew would claim his three bob, then call for a charity collecting box and ostentatiously post it in just to show what he thought of it.

"With bargemen's overtime then coming so cheap, it was a common practice to "knock off" a lighter at 5 p.m. and put a barge in its place to save the greater expense of keeping a lighterman on overtime. Or so it seemed in practice, whatever the ostensible reason was. But about five years ago an overtime rate of 15/- became payable for work up to 7 p.m.

"Now that it takes longer to get loaded or discharged, the motor barge takes longer to complete a freight. Earnings suffer accordingly, and earnings fluctuate anyway, since a bargeman is paid freightage and not a fixed wage."

There are two sides to every problem, however, and before registration dockers led an uneasy existence. Men used to queue outside the gates to the Connaught Entrance of the Royal Docks waiting to be taken on.

The long hours spent waiting, loading and unloading gave bargemen little time for themselves or for attending to their barge. Washing had to be done, water and food fetched. Taps and shops were always some distance away. Keeping the barge clean in dock was a virtual impossibility; note the dust spattered over *Edith May's* hull, in Plate 95, which shows her under the elevator. It was not until the barge locked-out into the tideway that she was able to shake free the dirt of this City of Ships.

One bargemate told me how time was found to do some washing under a dockside tap. The washing was being rinsed out when there were footsteps, and half turning round the mate was confronted by a pair of highly polished policeman's boots.

"And what do you think you're doing?" enquired the copper, rudely.

"My washing."

"Why?"

The mate fought to retain self-control. "Well look at it this way. You're a policeman and when your clothes get dirty, you wash them, right?"

"Right."

"Well bargemen get their clothes dirty, same as policemen!"

The copper wandered off, feeling perhaps that he might have lost that round.

Patricia reminded me that people ashore take water for granted: it is something which comes out of a tap.

"For the bargeman, the problem is getting *at* a tap, as a barge's supply is contained in a tank or tanks, and filling these can assume the proportions of a major operation. Yet one dare not let the supply get low, as one might have to spend several days weatherbound in a remote anchorage. For this reason barges often carried a small wooden cask, known as a barrico, which was always taken ashore in the bargeboat to be filled and used to keep the tank topped-up (Plate 148).

"There are facilities for obtaining fresh water in the docks, but

Plate 88c. Aboard *Edith May* . . . left Dilbury Clark who formerly maintained Brown's timber lighters. (Picture Stanley Cook).

these are designed with ships in mind, and are virtually useless for a small craft. To start with, an appointment has to be made, and a P.L.A. man comes along with a canvas hose, removes a manhole cover, connects up the hose and turns the supply on with a long key. The fact that an appointment has to be made complicates the issue. There are no designed lay berths for barges, only places where one is less likely to be disturbed than others, so a barge is always liable to be shifted at very short notice.

"This means that other sources have to be used, and an experienced mate had to know the position of all likely taps. There used to be more around when there were steam cranes, and some

Plate 89. Among the rattle and banter of London River . . . barges in the rearground against London Bridge. The steamers in the midground are the Billingsgate carrier ships which brought fish to the market from the North Sea trawler fleets. (Picture Bishopsgate Institute).

still remain, if you know where to look for them.

"So getting water generally involved walking to and fro carrying buckets, the contents being poured down a large funnel stuck in the deck opening which gave access to the water tank. In the *Northdown* there was no deck fitting, so the only way to fill the foc's'le tank was via the funnel, with the end jammed into a 4-foot length of hose-pipe which was in turn stuck into the filler-hole of the tank, which was behind the access ladder. The funnel had to be kept upright by two bits of spunyarn lashed to projections on either side of the foc's'le hatch.

"When one speaks to men who were bargeing before the war,

Plate 90. Way down the Estuary among the swatchways or marshlands . . . working up Faversham Creek on the first of the tide. (Picture John Cotton).

Plate 91. The cabin of Cremer's *Edith* of Rochester, showing the back of the settee and the wide after lockers which were known as the "Yarmouth Roads". *Edith's* lockers had hexagonal cut-glass knobs in place of the more usual brass ones. The cabin lamp is of brass in an iron frame. (Picture Patricia O'Driscoll).

Plate 92. The for'ard end of *Memory's* cabin. On the left is the companion ladder leading up to the scuttleway. The ladder was set in a small lobby behind a fold-back door (out of sight on the left). In the centre is the fresh-water tap which had an uncontrollable leak, hence the drip tray underneath. On the right is the cabin stove. (Picture Patricia O'Driscoll).

one realizes what a great improvement the war brought about in conditions for seamen in general, and also for dock workers. I have been told that the provision of canteens was a war-time measure, and as these could be used by all who worked in the docks, a number of bargemen got their dinner there. Although barges are residential craft, equipped with a stove and cooking utensils, there is not always time to prepare a meal if one is loading, tallying or shifting about, even if the mate is well-organized, and there were a number employed in that capacity who could hardly be trusted to make tea.

"Even after the war, the crew could still be expected to discharge cargo, generally with the aid of the mast-case winches or the dolly winch (shifted to the fore coaming). These were known as "handraulic" winches. Cranes being expensive, human effort was employed for unloading cargo as a matter of course. Which came hard on the crew, who might have been loading in the docks one day, then sailing all night if the wind was favourable, so they had done more of their share of work already without being expected to discharge their own cargo on arrival. Before the war, freights were hard to come by, and there were many owner/skippers struggling to make a bare living, which is one of the reasons why this custom lasted as long as it did.

Plate 93. Dockwork . . . Everard's *Cambria* alongside in the KGV entrance. (Picture Patricia O'Driscoll).

Plate 94. Dockers trimming coal . . . a cargo of "all or nothing", either large lumps or dust. (Picture Keystone, from the Conway Picture Library).

"Timber cargoes were taken ashore by other labour, but the crew was required to stand the timber on end to assist the gang. Extra heavy timber had to be slung ashore (by the crew), with the aid of the barge's gear. Fortunately the situation has altered, and to be asked to discharge cargo is now very unusual in most places. So life for the crew has improved by that much anyway from the "good old days"."

If dockwork was refractory, the sailorman accepted it with a grudging forbearance characteristic of his logic, in the same way he once accepted the gruelling task of working above bridges.

The barges worked up, under their own power, as far as Putney,

Plate 95. Alongside the elevator in the Victoria Dock . . . *Edith May* loading 133 tons of No 2 Manitoba wheat for Stambridge, ex *Loch Garth*. (Picture Patricia O'Driscoll).

and if working above there a tug had to be taken to Teddington, where there was a smaller tug available to take craft up through the locks. Before 1930 this was all done by horse-tow, and if working above Putney with ballast an extra 3d per yard was paid. Of course, there was a tug available all the way up from the Pool, but no one could afford it.

For canal work barges were designed to fit into the locks—just. But leeboards had to be removed, though boat and anchor stowed inboard, and then there was no room to accommodate a barge and a fender. *E.F.Q.* locked-in one day.

"Don't put that fender in" ordered her Master, but it was too late. It wedged and took her crew half an hour to cut it out.

There were tunnels to be negotiated on the Regent's Canal system. At one time these were worked by "legging", the crew lying on their backs on the hatches with their feet up against the tunnel roof. Later a coke-burning tug was employed. One Skipper remembered that the stench from the funnel was so great that he had to retire to his cabin for the duration of the tow. Eastwood's craft took cement up to Providence Wharf for the building of Wembley Stadium. Now to get a barge's head down under the tunnel roofs, the barge boat was placed on the forehatch and filled with water. One of the barges bound up with cement for Wembley struck against the roof.

"It weren't my fault," the then mate recalled. "It were the skipper's; 'e forgot ter fill the boat up!"

Horlock's later barges were constructed of Dutch-Iron and built to carry acids to Bow Creek, *Repertor* having a ballast tank built under the fo'c'sle ceiling which could be filled again so that the head could be got down. Another tight fit was through the bridges leading up to Colchester's East Mills where the barges lowered down to be poked up into the lovely basin almost in the centre of the town. *Millie* went up one day, touched under one of the bridges, and could only be freed by her crew cutting a few inches off the top of her bittheads.

After unloading bricks at the various destinations above bridges the Kentishmen used to look for a return freight of London rubbish which was used in the brickfields. It was the practice for a barge to anchor off a wharf and for the skipper to row ashore and enquire if there was a freight.

Once clear of the bridges the gear was hove up and the barge could be made ship-shape again. With a good breeze a smart barge could be away from the Pool on the first of the ebb and be down off the Nore ready to take the young flood up the Medway. Sea Reach was a nasty place for little barges in a blow. If it cut up rough, the usual place to lie was in the Hope near the powder barges at the entrance to Sea Reach and if bound "down Swin", the East Anglian barges when caught out, ran back to lie under the lee of Southend Jetty. Horlock's *Xylonite*, now a motor barge, was caught out in the 1953 floods off the Jetty. Billy Hamilton who was then Mate with Theo Horlock, told me that they laid out every link of chain and let the barge lie, retiring to their cabin for three days.

Plate 96. Stowing woodpulp in the after cupboard of *Olive May* in the Surrey. (Picture Patricia O'Driscoll).

Caught-out in the Swin, a barge would attempt to get into the Colne or the Blackwater, or if it was not possible to cross the Spitways she would lie-to in Abraham's Bosom. The sands on the Spitways are rock-hard and grounding could be a terrifying experience. The Kentishmen had no such shelter so they sailed "wet or dry". Their maxim was: "if you could get down you went down"

In comparison to other sailing craft, a barge is able to stand up to heavy weather, but the East Coast is a vicious place in a grumpy sea and strong wind.

In *Repertor* we once loaded 125 tons of sulphate of ammonia at East Greenwich for Ipswich, going down with *Resourceful* to lie just below Queenborough Hard to escape a Force 7 blow. After two days the wind started Force 6, S.S.E., lulled, and the weather-man promised us easier weather. We mustered, taking three hours ebb over the Spitways into the Wallet Channel. *Veravia* thundered past us, bound up light, and throwing plumes of spray down her side; it was evident that the promised lull was not be. Indeed the wind freshened almost as soon as we got over the Spitways. At 3 p.m. we were rolling heavily off Clacton Pier—an hour later we were still there—making no way, and setting the tops'l to try and drive that big barge down over the tide. With decks awash, the seas sometimes knocking the wedges out of their battens we staggered through the Rolling Grounds, while our former friend, the weatherman, told us we could now expect to experience Gale Force 8 conditions. After a twelve hour passage we were peering through the spray to find the leading lights into Harwich Harbour— a gybe—and we rushed in past the Beach End buoy to anchor off Stone Heaps. That night we listened to a severe gale.

Those big steel barges could take heavy weather though, but in the moments of our passage I had a brief insight into what life must have been like in some of the older, sparsely fitted-out craft, which loaded right up to and sometimes over their rubbing bands, sailing with two men at the wheel or pumping to keep afloat.

So often barges got into trouble by stranding, collision, founder-

Plate 97. *Cambria* **winching over by means of the dolly onto Bellamy's Wharf, Southwark, to load from ss** *Pinemore* **(Picture Patricia O'Driscoll).**

Plate 98. Working above bridges . . . swim-headers at Aylesford on the upper Medway. (Picture Alan Cordell Collection).

ing or just breaking gear in heavy weather, but because of their construction many were able to be salved. The sight of a barge wreck was not unusual. In 1920, *Opal* anchored off Margate in heavy seas, rolling badly, and the Margate lifeboat was launched to rescue her crew of two, but during the night the vessel sank. Later the hull was blown up but first the wrecked vessel's gear was torn out. Tom Redshaw remembers seeing her off Margate that last night. He was ten years of age.

Ironsides had two narrow escapes. In 1902 she sank in collision with SS. *Ophelia* off Limehouse with a cargo of hides and bamboo; and then in October 1929 the Dungeness lifeboat took off her crew of two. The Peck-built boomie *Ethel Edith* also had her crew of five plus a woman taken off by lifeboat, when she started to leak badly on passage with china clay from Par to Dagenham in 1933. Inevitably the sea took its toll of life. When the *Cecil Rhodes* grounded under Warden Cliffs in 1911 the coastguard, Mr William Hall, was able to rescue Captain F. Baker, but Cecil Hoare, the mate, was lost. Mr Hall was later decorated for his bravery. Another coastguard to be so decorated saved the lives of the crew of Goldsmith's *Astrild* which, running for shelter clay-laden out of Poole, stranded at Folkestone in 1907. It was thought at first that the barge would become a total loss, but surprisingly she refloated the following day and survived a second time when her crew was taken off by the Aldeburgh lifeboat during the terrible gale of 23rd November 1938. The barge, abandoned, strayed across to Holland. It was the crew of another Goldsmith barge, *Briton*, who came across the *Esther* foundering in Sea Reach. Her master had taken to the rigging, and Captain Thomas Ambrose, with his mate Edgar Davies, launched *Briton's* boat in the height of an E.S.E. gale to rescue him. *Pudge's* crew of three were saved off the Chapman when the barge was in collision with the (G.S.N. Co's) SS *Lapwing* in 1935; *Thyra's* crew was taken off in 1933, and the Ipswich *Tollesbury* came into difficulty no less than three times.

In Chapter III Percy Brown described how *Lord Lansdowne* was caught out, an instance which I think occurred in 1912. Now that barge was notorious for getting into trouble. She was evidently a regular trader to the Tyne with scrap metals, for in 1905 returning from South Shields to Rye with coal, she drove ashore between Rye and Winchelsea. Salved, she was soon off back to the Tyne again, and two years later, laden with scrap rails, she was towed

Plate 102. The East Coast is a vicious place in a grumpy sea and a strong wind . . . *Ethel Maud* deep-laden in the Swin. (Picture Patricia O'Driscoll).

into Scarborough disabled. Once before, in 1900, she had been in collision.

Collisions between two barges were fortunately infrequent. Two instances, however, were when *Tollesbury* rammed the Weymouth-owned *Challenge* in 1909, and suffered a broken sprit and topmast; and when *British King* and *Savoy* struck in 1935.

Capsizes, too, were rare. One mystery concerned the Ipswich *Robert Powell* which loaded stone in 1907 at Cherbourg for Folkestone. Soon afterwards she was sighted floating bottom upwards off the French coast, and on 20th January was washed ashore one mile to the east of Newhaven. Presumably her cargo had shifted but her crew were never found. Righted on 27th January she was rebuilt at Ipswich as the *Wolsey*, and two years later lost her topmast "down Channel" when laden with "patent manure".

Working confined waterways, especially the narrow coastal creeks, was always difficult. Wills & Packham's *Company* used to work to Teddington and one day she went right over the weir and was smashed up. It is said that Smeed Dean's bought the wreck afterwards and rebuilt it.

In contrast, there was nothing more frustrating to a bargeman than to be becalmed. Being windbound, waiting for a favourable slant was excusable, but to be becalmed when everyone else in the river had a puff of wind was too much. Sailormen still believe that some of their number are able to conjure up wind. The art of trolling, as it is called, probably had Nordic origins, and it was done by sticking a knife in the mast, by whistling, by murmuring incantations, or by throwing a sum of money overboard to buy wind. In these ways, the "line managers" as old sailors called the wind gods, were invoked to improve matters in the particular vicinity of the craft.

There is, however, a saying that "when you buy wind, you also buy its burden" and like hot-air ballooning, the results are entirely unpredictable. Certainly, no one admits there is any credibility to trolling—it is just that nobody does it, at least not often. Stafford Pitt did it once. He chucked a half-penny over the stern on a perfectly calm day. The look on the skipper's face afterwards was enough to discourage its repetition. It blew alright—perhaps it was coincidence—but when the topmast snapped we began to wonder!

Alan Cordell recalls that his grandfather, James Fenteman, was a firm believer, as were many old-time bargemen, and would never resort to bad language or blasphemy. Better, he thought, to raise a wind by throwing a penny over the side. In an uncharacteristic fit of sheer reckless generosity Jim once threw *two* pennies over *Yieldsted's* side. He brought the barge home dismasted!

Plate 104. The "mulie" *Challenge* of Weymouth entering harbour. The mate is standing by the mastcase and has just let go the tops'l halyard to ruck that sail. (Picture from the Collection of the Late Mr E. Latcham).

Chapter V
ONE MAN'S FLEET

There are great barge owning families who are able to trace the origin of their interests back a century or even a century and a half ago, a span encompassing almost the entire history of the sprits'l barge. Some, owning barges not so many years ago, like Rankin, Sadd, Gill and Shrubsall, had owned them when the sloop and the cutter were the common rigs in the estuary.

It is interesting to delve into the early beginnings of some of the barge families. I say families because there was a strong element of family participation and continuation on the East Coast. The building up of a fleet of sailing barges usually resulted from the impetus of one powerful man who might have started life either as a merchant or as a barge skipper, and had gradually expanded into ownership. As ownership was ancilliary to other business interests it would, a century ago, have been a cut-throat business. A man owned ships for profit and the age produced remarkable individuals. There was Edward Fairbrass the hoyman, who came to own a great fleet of brigs and schooners; William Charles Murrell's fortune came from carting away London refuse; Osborne Dan, when one of his crews gave him trouble, once sailed the barge up to London with a brace of pistols in his belt during a bargemen's strike of the 1890's; and then there was George John Vandervord who enjoyed a marked preference for litigation.

Let us look now at some of the barge fleets which men like these built up.

"Zachariah Crabb married Elizabeth Jolly on the 9th August 1768. . . ." So begins Nigel Halsey's note to me on his family history, and from this union stemmed the beginnings of the Rankin's of Broomhills River. It was their eldest daughter Elizabeth who married William Rankin, a Bocking farmer, to whom a son, William Hugh, was born in 1800. He married his cousin Jane 27 years later, moving to Stambridge where in 1824 the Rankin and Tabor families had entered in business together as millers, farmers, corn and coal merchants. Young Rankin took a lease from Charterhouse on the water and wind mill, the former being the 'new' mill built in 1762. The wind mill was rebuilt in 1814 to replace the old one previously sited at Rochford. This had formerly been leased to the Herriot family, whose son George became one of the co-founders of the Thames River Police.

The partnership formed between William Hugh and his second cousin Samuel Tabor was to last for just over 20 years. Stambridge

Plate 105. Stambridge Mill yesterday and the day before. Above: The mill in the 1930's. The brick building to the right of the tide mill was the old office, replaced in 1939 by a new office in Mill Lane. (Picture by Courtesy of N. C. Halsey).
Below: (L) Auxiliary *Varuna*, (C) *Lord Roberts*, and (R) *Edith May* at the mill. The weather-boarded tide mill on the left caught fire in the 1960's. (Picture Patricia O'Driscoll).

then was quite a busy little port with two hoy barges, the *Hope* and the *Four Brothers*, with a ship chandler's shop and a sail-maker's loft. Probably Rankin himself owned these hoys, for in 1848 he was described as a barge owner, corn and coal merchant.

Of William Hugh Rankin's fifteen children, two sons, Alfred and Hugh, joined him in business, converting the mill to steam power in 1869.

By the 1860's the two hoys had been disposed of and the family purchased the then nearly new sprits'l barge *Surprise* from Smee at Maldon. This barge maintained the Stambridge hoy service until the early 1900's when she was sold to Curtis & Harvey, and was replaced by the *Lord Roberts* which was bought from Meeson. After *Surprise* the family acquired the Sunderland-built schooner

Ellen, a sturdy 100 ton craft which 70 years after her building was at work for Lancashire owners. Plate 107 shows her ketch rigged at Faversham when owned in that port by Chas Marshall, the draper, who had interests in a number of barges. In 1914 *Lord Roberts* was joined by the newly built *Joy*, from Alfred White's yard at Conyer, and the two barges worked to the Stambridge mill for nearly 40 years, until *Joy* was sold to become a yacht, ending up in the Mediterranean, while the former became an auxiliary, then a motor barge, and was finally re-rigged as a yacht by Tony Winter.

In 1847 the fortunes of the Rankin family became entwined with those of the Meeson's. William Taylor Meeson, who came from Grays in the 1830's, went to Battlesbridge where he owned the tide mill together with farms at Rettendon, Paglesham and Rochford. The family were also barge owners at Grays where his brother was one of the founders of the Grays Chalk Quarries Company. Meeson's produce was carried afloat by the barges *Vickers* and *Meeson*, under Captains Humphreys and Marsh. One of these called at Stambridge every Tuesday.

Henry Tabor, writing in his "Tabor Family History" published in 1917, describes Stambridge as he remembered it as a boy in the 1850's: "There was a wharf which was accessible to vessels of 100 or 120 tons of burden, such as Colliers as we called them, Brigs or schooners, bringing coal from Sunderland and Newcastle or more common 'Sprit. sail' barges. . . These took flour to Harvey and Napier's Junction Wharf whence it was carted to the London bakehouses. They also carried hay and straw piled on deck, *halfway up the mast*!"

Soon after this account was written Meeson acquired the elderly barge *Charlotte*, built in 1799, *Factor*, *Runwell*, and a schooner *Glencoe* which delivered coal to Battlesbridge on the springs, and to Barling Quay when the tides were neap. These were joined in the 1860's by three new barges from Milton, *Rawreth*, *Roache* and *Rettendon*, and later *Sarah & Helen*, *Paglesham*, the Howard built boomie *Malvoisin*, which later joined *Ellen* in Marshall's Faversham fleet, the little stumpy *Rainbow*, and finally Joe Mizzen's old Lambeth built *James*.

There was plenty of work for the barges in these waters for this was among the best farmland in the country, where freeholds could fetch at the best £20 per acre, and "lookers" were paid 15/-. per week. "Looker" was the local name for a farm labourer, who in the harvest month could expect to receive 135/-. plus an allowance of malt and hops. By way of comparison the railway porter at nearby Southminster around the turn of the century received only 1/-. per week more. No doubt the barge skipper who earned between 20/-. and 30/-. a week was considered to be quite well off.

One family who ran an occasional hoy service which took in Stambridge were the Vandervords of Southend. The three brothers, George who was master of the *Royal Oak*, James who was master of the *Minerva* and William who was master of the *Waterloo*, appear to have acquired these craft on the death of their father Abraham when his estate went to auction.

The brothers were by all accounts a fairly rough trio, their

Plate 106. The Rankins of Broomhills River. Above: William H. Rankin, born 1800, died 1872; barge owner, corn and coal merchant. Below: His son Hugh Rankin, born 1842, died 1922, pictured the year before his death. (Pictures by Courtesy of N. C. Halsey).

Plate 107. Two of the Rankin family ships. Above: The ketch *Ellen*, shown at Faversham around 1900 when she had been sold to Marshall of that port (Picture by Courtesy of John Cotton and Robin Partis). Right: *Lord Roberts*. (Picture Les Arnold).

ensuing legal wrangles stemming from the time of an appeal assessed on them in respect of rates and charges on the *Royal Oak* and the *Minerva*. The Notice of Appeal served on Prittlewell on the 2nd of July 1819 contended that the "Rate or Assessment is unequal illegal and unjust upon us" and went on to claim that other owners in the parish were omitted to be rated. Hervey Benham in "Down Tops'l" relates the famous incident when the Vandervords tried to evade payment of tolls in the 1830's for landing goods at the newly built Southend pier and along the shore within three miles of the Pier Hotel, by inciting local watermen to break down the pier toll gate. The pier company collector attempted to distrain on the family goods. I do not know the cost of the tolls disputed but it must have been minimal in comparison to the costs incurred by the family's solicitor. The rendered account ran to many pages, detailing such items as "Boat hire and expenses to Southend (half) at 4/3d." and to serving subpoenas at 5/-. each on William Hay, Joseph Pritchard, Captains Brusier (misprinted for Brasier), Harland and Cranfield, and on Thomas Pritchard the Southend pilot. The solicitor lost out on one gentleman for I find an item of only 6d. for "Copy subpoena for service on Mr Fox but he had left home to prevent this being served. . . ."

In all, this litigation seems to have involved a great number of people in and around Southend and from the accounts charged we are able to learn the names of many of the local merchants and officers of the time.

For a while a steam packet service from London was run by way of the *Sir Joseph Yorke* which from approximately 1823 to 1843 supplemented the Saturday hoy sailings. When George died in 1843 the continued litigation had caused the business to fall to a low ebb, but it was revived by his two sons George and Emmanuel, under whose partnership fortunes rose. A fourth barge *Emily* was acquired and in 1850 we find her at Poplar where Chapman Vandervord writes that they "Will get all their wheat out today and he (a reference presumably to Sam the master) wants to go up with potatoes tomorrow."

In 1857 James erected a stage or jetty opposite the Ship Tavern for the purpose of unloading and loading corn and other goods at a cost of three hundred pounds. Two years later he made an agreement with young George and Emmanuel that he would convey his business of hoyman together with barges, boats, horses, waggons, carts, stock stores etc., to them for the consideration of two thousand pounds, agreeing to recommend them to all late or present customers and contracting not to enter into the business of hoyman at Southend or within a space of 20 miles thereof under the penalty or sum of £500.

Long before the three elder brothers had acquired their father's estate, their grandfather, also called Abraham, had been hoyman at Leigh back in the middle of the 18th century, buying from one George Richardson for the sum of "five hundred pounds of lawful money of Great Britain" the sloop *Mary & Elizabeth* in 1744. Abraham married for the 4th. time in 1756, and at the age of 70 produced a son who 18 years later became master of the *Pitsea*.

Plate 108. Working up in a calm under sweeps. The crews of the brick and cement barges were powerful men. They loaded their own freights and propelled their craft up narrow waterways when the wind was foul or calm. Here the skipper and mate of the *Clipper* are seen rowing by means of the enormous oars known as sweeps. (Picture M. A. Farnham Collection).

In the 19th century the family came to own a granary at Southend and to extend their fleet to around 9 sprits'l barges. These included two iron pots *John Evelyn* and *Rathbale*, and the 20 ton booms'l barge *Assistance*. It was *Rathbale* which in August 1899 was lying at Nieuport when her Master posted a letter to his employers on the Wednesday evening. The barge arrived back at Southend at 10 p.m. on the Thursday while the letter followed, to arrive on the Friday morning. The *Essex Weekly News* gleefully recorded the event asking what the Postmaster General had to say about that, and pointing out that the barge which thus beat Her Majesty's mail was laden with bricks!.

It was shortly after this that Alfred disposed of the barges and the family business to Goldsmiths, with the exception of his favourite barge *Jane* which he retained until 1919, according to the registers. I notice that in 1912 *Jane* took a freight of barrelled herring from Grimsby to Ostende and that she had to be helped into Broadstairs in heavy weather. Her master at the time was Captain Markham, and I wonder if this was the Captain Markham who had *Coombdale* when later he made Ramsgate with a broken rudder head.

In the 1830's when William Hugh Rankin was shipping flour and corn to London and the Vandervord's hoy service ran from Pickle Herring Upper Wharf in Tooley Street (it was George Vandervord who married a Horsley-down girl in 1814) John Eastwood was busy founding his brickmaking business. In time it became a national concern, nearly 80 barges passing through the company's ownership.

Under his sons John and William the business became a private limited company in 1872, brickfields having been established at Shoebury, Rainham, Newington, Sittingbourne, Faversham, Lower Halstow and at various places inland. These produced all types of bricks, tiles and pipes, averaging an output around the turn of the century of 70 million bricks a year. A fleet of sailing barges was built up to carry the bricks from the fields to the depots at Lambeth, Bermondsey, Chelsea, Mortlake, Clapton, Paddington, Richmond and Weybridge (Plate 112).

Other interests, including barges, were acquired from an amalgamation with other manufacturers, one of whom, Rowley Richardson, brought in with him the Conyer cement works. In 1892 the company employed Ambrose Letley to build for them a 39 ton tops'l barge at the Halstow yard they had acquired, the *Whaup*, although two years previously he had built *Grebe* for Quilter, and the following year Letley began work on *Lapwing*. At the same time the Whites were commissioned to build a series of barges which included *Alpha*, *Durham* and *Westmoreland*. The latter was donated to the T.B.S.C. in 1963, while *Durham* ended her working life as a mud lighter in the 1950's, gaff-rigged. In 1899 Eastwoods took over R. M. Shrubsall's Sittingbourne yard where they built *Bedford* (Plate 111) among other craft, before finally opening a repair yard at Otterham in 1912. The first barge to be housed in the shed at Otterham was *Sigma* which had had her stern cut off.

Plate 109. A Southend hoyman . . . Emmanuel Vandervord was born on 18th August 1829 and was taken into partnership by his brother George upon the death of their mother in 1851. (Picture by Courtesy of Mrs V. Vandervord).

Generally the barges were named after birds, Greek letters of the alphabet and English counties. Mr Percy Cook, who served the firm for 53 years, remembered that at one time they owned approximately 53 craft (possibly an underestimation), distinguishable by the words EASTWOODS BRICKMAKERS emblazoned on their sails. Some like *Surrey* were stump rigged for up-river work. Soon after the Great War it was realised that with the coming of the motor lorry it would be impossible to keep sailing barges going on a profitable basis, so the fleet was gradually reduced in number until by the outset of the last war many of them had been laid up, later to do duty as powder hulks in the Medway creeks.

The stump rig was a favourite one for the brick and cement trades. These were the workhorses of the tideway, heavy to handle but not substantially slower than their tops'l sisters. Their great advantage lay in the ease with which their gear could be lowered, and as there was no topmast to be dropped they were popular with owners on the Medway above Rochester and Aylesford bridges. William Lee & Co, cement manufacturers at Halling, owned a fleet of them which in the early years of the Thames and Medway barge races dominated the Spritsail Class, collecting no less than 18 racing trophies. As the winning barge in the Spritsail Class was unable to compete in that class the following year their champion barge *Invicta* was sometimes rigged tops'l in alternate years and came home first in the Tops'l Class of the Thames race in 1868. Stumpies were owned in numbers by Peters of Wouldham, by Woods of Sittingbourne, whose *Columbus*, *Kalulu*, *Volante* and *Frances* brought explosives ingredients to the Swale powder factories, by Hilton, Anderson & Brooks from their Upnor and Faversham mills, and by the Burham Brick, Lime and Cement Company. Rutters owned a few at Great Wakering, and at the near-by Stambridge brickworks Featherby owned *Bessie*, *Formosa* and *Millie*, but the best remembered were those owned at Murston by Smeed Dean.

Plate 110. *Westmoreland* **racing. (Picture Patricia O'Driscoll).**

George W. Smeed began shipowning with a collection of ketch and schooner rigged collier barges, turning after amalgamation with George Hambrook Dean to brick and cement production. Joe Hines who is historian to the Society for Spritsail Barge Research has assessed that 153 craft were at one time or another owned by the company. The Murston Cement Works was purchased from the Burham Brick, Lime and Cement Company, some of whose barges were *January*, *May* and *June*.

All carried the letters BCᵒ in their sails. Cement for the building of Smeed Dean's new works at Murston was carried from the old Turkey Cement Works at Elmley on the Swale. Captain Fenteman, when master of the *Wave*, took away the very first freight of bricks from the new brickworks at Murston in the 1880's.

The firm looked after their barges with extraordinary care even to the extent that their craft were rebuilt instead of being doubled when they showed signs of age. Once a year each barge went onto the yard at Murston where the closest attention was paid to the hull, rigging and sails. It was estimated that a mains'l enjoyed a life of 11 years.

To keep the sails in order a number of sailmakers were employed and at one period each barge had a sail number marked on her canvas, *Gladstone's* number was 49 and *Lowe's* 31. Unfortunately, around 1900, the firm took on a rather poor sailmaker who is said to have caused them a lot of trouble, for if he could not easily get his needle through the canvas he would tack the bolt rope to the sail with wire nails, often tacking canvas round a worn piece of boltrope rather than replacing it! The late Captain Kennett recalled: "They were queer old sails, they were high-peaked, and the leech was like a rainbow. It was as if you were underway with half a sail!". After him the firm's sailmakers were young Mr Clarke and in the 1920's a Mr Prentice.

Unlike many barges the Smeed Dean fleet did not have to seek their own freights; they were all arranged by the company, and it was seldom that a barge left a port light laden. At Milton Creek with so many craft entering and leaving on each tide there was a system in operation for the berthing of each craft as it came up the creek. In charge of berthing, at one time, was the foreman Charles Shilling. The barges brought up in the creek and it was a rule that the mate of the first barge to enter sculled ashore and walked up to Charles' cottage to receive the berthing orders for all the others. As foreman he was on duty seven days and nights a week but is said never to have complained at being woken up at all hours of the night.

One of smallest of the Murston barges was *Sam*, which worked to Tottenham and to Weybridge where she could carry only 28,000 bricks, while the largest of the sprits'l barges, bar *Hydrogen* in which I think the firm only had a share, was the fine coaster *Youngarth*.

Youngarth was the last barge to be built at Murston and was bowsprit rigged for Channel work. In contrast to *Sam* she once loaded 70,000 bricks for Barking Creek. Her master was Tom Pearce who was commonly regarded as being the Commodore

Plate 111. Eastwood's *Bedford* deep-laden in London River. (Picture by Courtesy of Alan Cordell).

Skipper of the fleet, taking her new-built from the yard in 1913. The barge worked mainly down to the South Coast, bringing back china clay from Poole and Wareham, with the occasional trip to Yarmouth and Ipswich. On one trip they met what was to them a quite unusual barge, steel and by far the largest sprits'l barge they had ever seen. Later the crew were to learn that this leviathan was the newly built *Will Everard*. "She was sailing light at the time," *Youngarth's* Mate recalled, "Through the Solent, and we reckoned that she was a bit crank, but no doubt she sailed well deep laden."

On their way back from Ipswich or Yarmouth the barges were directed to pick up sand from Brightlingsea beach. The beach was an uncomfortable place to lie, being very exposed, and berthing was an uneasy experience. On arrival in the Colne the crew would look out for the marks on the beach, two wheelbarrows and a withy, the latter marking the spot where the leeboard was to lie.

Thirty yards off the beach the barge would drop her anchor short and the mate would scull ashore with a line to the wheelbarrow off the bow. This would then be dug into the shingle and a bow rope made fast to the wheel. He would row back to the barge for the stern line and the procedure was repeated with the second wheelbarrow. The barge would then be warped in.

Plate 112. Eastwood's *Surrey*, a stumpy, at Weybridge in 1925 (Picture Alan Cordell Collection).

90

In a heavy swell both skipper and mate would be required to row and on one occasion *Youngarth's* boat capsized and Tom Pearce with his mate, "Chippy" Wood was flung into the water. Both reached the beach safely and righted the boat. Tom had his wife and daughter aboard and both were nearly sick with worry watching the incident. "Chippy" remembers that the daughter had to be revived with brandy afterwards.

On another occasion *Youngarth* was up at Ipswich with grain, but in this case it was the mate of one of Piper's barges who got wet.

The practice at Ipswich was to come up and tie on the buoys in front of the lock gates and wait there until the lock-in. The buoys were sited close to the gates and if a barge came up too hard she risked hitting the dock wall. Piper's barge came up under skipper "Shanker Bill" and was obviously carrying too much way, and instead of being able to lean over the side and loop the mooring rope through the eye the mate had to jump for the buoy. As soon as the mooring rope was fast the skipper took a turn and immediately the buoy started to revolve. The mate began to do a little dance, trying to keep his balance on the impromptu round-about, and at the same time jump over the taut rope every time he came round.

Soon the mate fell in, and on seeing there was no danger "Shanker Bill" began to laugh, while his mate, swimming back to his barge, shouted all manner of rude phrases back to him.

Smeed Dean's bricks were hand made, sand-yellow in colour, and had the initials S.D. stamped on their frogs. These were known as stocks and were very popular for housebuilding and for factories. Stocks harden over the years and now that there is a shortage of new bricks second-hand stocks are sometimes used for housebuilding, and being set in lime mortar the older bricks are easy to scrape clean. I have one before me as I write—a very ordinary brick. I was visiting a building site overlooking the sea at Westgate when a lorry arrived with a load of second-hand Smeed Dean stocks, which had come from a house which had just been demolished in London, and which were to be used for the building of a new estate. Originally, my brick had gone up to London by barge before the turn of the century.

Bricks were made by gangs, and the chief man in the team was the moulder. At Murston a gang sometimes manufactured a million "green" bricks in a season, and if this was achieved a ceremony was held. First a flag was run up on the roof of the shed and then the moulder broke the bowl off his pipe and inserted it into the body of the millionth brick.

A builder named Jack Monk recently picked up a brick to clean it when it snapped in half. Nestling inside was the bowl of a clay pipe.

In 1933 Smeed Dean amalgamated with the A.P.C.M. "combine" when 52 of their barges were taken over. Not long after this APCM started to sell off many of them and some were sold for as little as £1 per registered ton.

Murston today looks very forlorn. The old blocks have gone,

although they were there until recently. Parts of the site are being demolished and the old Murston gas works stands very much alone. Through lack of usage the banks of the creek have silted up, while the wharves—like Uncle Tom's, Barn Berth, Marsh Berth and Slop Berth—have almost crumbled away. Near the Marsh Berth lies the remains of the "little" *Gladstone*, another "cut" barge, sunk into the mud almost up to her covering boards. Now it seems unbelievable that in 1894 there were no less than 304 Milton Creek built barges then still afloat.

We started this chapter with the rivers Crouch and Roach—let's return to them.

Although the land surrounding these rivers was so predominantly agricultural there were, a hundred years ago, around 35 barges, four schooners and a West Country built barquentine, the *Saint Brannock*, owned on just these two rivers, not counting the craft owned around Foulness and Wakering. Burnham had become established as a port during the Middle Ages when pilgrims landed there on their way to the shrine at Walsingham. The Hawkins family came to have an important quay at the town, and for nearly one and a half centuries they were hoymen there, with craft like the *Endeavour*, *Crouch*, which was their last barge, and the very famous hoy *Good Intent*, which was built in 1790 and was still

Plate 113. Lower Halstow taken from the brickfields bank. The stumpy *Mistletoe* is seen in front of the attractive marshland church of St. Margaret of Antioch, whose structure contains some Roman brickwork. (Picture Alan Cordell Collection).

working in the early years of the 20th century. Two other well-known craft here were the little schooner *Minerva*, owned by Richmond the coal merchant, and the jackass schooner barge *Lucy Richmond* which was the pride of Burnham River. That barge was broken up at Cubitt Town in 1940, and her enormous main-mast was built into the face of Piper's Wharf at East Greenwich.

Burnham's most famous ship was Benjamin Cackett's Hullbridge owned *Triumph*. Both Hullbridge and Fambridge were the sites of former bridges and both came to have small wharves. *Triumph* was actually built at Hullbridge, where Cackett owned a fleet of aged sprits'l barges, among them *Hopewell* (1803) and *Maltster* (1807), which were used to carry lime and chalk up as far as Battlesbridge. Incredible as it seems *Triumph* was only 61 regis-tered Tons, yet she once voyaged across the Atlantic in the 1880's. Then in 1887 she arrived at Greenwich to be rebuilt as the sprits'l barge *Coombdale*. This was not the end of her exciting life. In 1906 she sank off Woolwich after being in collision with SS *Player*; then she was sold to Theobalds and on passage to Dieppe broke her rudder head. Her master, Captain Markham, managed to fetch Ramsgate without assistance, and repairs completed, the barge continued her voyage. For a while she came to be owned in Dundee, finally being hulked on Cliffe Marshes around the age of 100.

Plate 114. Wood's stumpy *Columbus* under way in Milton Creek. The barge on the left alongside Wills & Pack-ham's quay is either *Edward* or *Medway*. Barges had been built here at Crown Quay since the 1790's. (Picture Alan Cordell Collection).

93

The men who built up these great fleets of barges might have been rough and hard people, but then the world that they operated in was also hard. A few of them resorted to sharp practices, yet were capable of showing great generosity to their crews, sometimes providing them with cottages ashore and pensions on retirement. There were men like Charles Cremer who was deeply religious, and like Hugh Rankin, on whose death all Stambridge mourned.

Hugh Rankin's daughter, Joan Halsey, wrote a poem in his memory, which my colleague Colin Edgar found recently written on the flyleaf of a book "By Rochford Town", written by Sir Alfred Temple:

"The Stambridge Miller Passes"
In memory of the late Mr Hugh Rankin

"The Stambridge Mill has a charm for me
  With its wide salt river not far from the sea
And the barges sailing up on the tide
  To unload and anchor close to the side
Of the dear old ancient Mill.

The Miller, himself, has daily gone
  Down to the place where he was born
Where his father and mother lived and died
  In this beautiful home by the riverside
In Stambridge down by the Mill.

For years and years he has passed this way
  We hoped he would for many a day
With his radiant face and sparkling eye
  And a greeting for all who passed him by
On his daily walk to the Mill.

But the cold East winds are bad, I fear
  For one who has passed his eightieth year.
"Give up and rest" said a friend he met.
  "Retire from work?" said he "Not yet."
"I must go down to the Mill."

"The Miller is not so well," they say
  But still we see him pass this way,
With shoulders bent and walking slow
  As to his daily work he'll go
Always down to the Mill.

But New Year's Eve was a day to mourn
  When the streets were hushed and the blinds were drawn
And many a friend with a tear or sigh,
  Did come to see him, passing by
For the last time down to the Mill."

Chapter VI
THE SHIPWRIGHT'S ART

There are few more satisfying sights than watching an expert craftsman going about his task. Add to this sight the enticing odours from a glue pot on the boil, a bucket of pitch bubbling, the indescribably piquant aroma from Stockholm Tar, plus the hissing from the steam chest boiler, the thud of an adze biting into timber and the result is that most elysian workshop —the barge repair yard. Here men take timbers and shape them by eye to fit the curving lines of a hull, perhaps working with the selfsame tools their grandfathers used before them.

The way in which craft are repaired has altered little over the years, for although timbers might now be roughly cut to shape on a bandsaw, and shipwrights no longer have to tap out their oak treenails through a "trunnel-plate", as Dick Norton recalls having done, much of the shipwright's work is still done by hand.

Plate 115 illustrates the scene in a yard shop. In the mid foreground is the steam chest boiler, with the steam chest above in which the larger hull planks are made pliable.

It is hard and patient work to keep a barge in sailing condition today, and it is fortunate that there are still yards where the heavier tasks can be carried out. After a half century or more of heavy treatment under trade many of a barge's timbers will need replacement. When decks and covering boards start to rot the continual water seepage will result in waterlogged frames and inner hull timbers. The only answer is to open the hull up, allow the timbers to dry out, then shape and fit replacements.

It is a necessary task, and one which Colin Frake and other members of the Thames Barge Sailing Club at Faversham are carrying out on *Westmoreland*. Now, new inwales and linings have been fitted from aft to just under the mast deck, laid on alternative frames which were slotted in. Parts of the wales, rails, covering board and decking have been relaid, and there are new beams and knees. The older timbers were scraped down and dried out before being treated with preservative. It has been slow work— and next year it is the for'ard part which will have to be attended to.

In 1972 Gordon Swift took time to show me round the barge repair yard at Maldon, where a big new shed has been built large enough to take a barge if necessary. In the centre of the shed a smack was up for repair; a pair of new leeboards were being shaped up in one corner (Plate 118) and a pole had been laid across trestles ready to be cut into a new topmast. On the blocks and grid, off the bank, were the barges *May*, up for her annual

Plate 115. The steam chest at Walter Cook & Sons Maldon yard in 1961. A fire was lit in the brick hearth, shown in the foreground, heating the water in a dome-shaped copper. On the left of the dome is the filler hole and on the right the pipe through which the steam was conducted into the chest. Planks were laid in the chest which was loosely sealed with old sacks at the open end to avoid a build up of pressure. The chest is elevated above the boiler. (Picture Patricia O'Driscoll).

Plate 116. The forest of masts and spars and steam tubs which is the Maldon waterfront. Foreground: *May* up on the ways, right centre: *Adriatic*. (Picture the Author).

refit, *Ethel*, which was being converted from a motor barge ready for a passage which was to take her round the West Coast to Liverpool and was having a new heel scarphed into her mainmast, and Gordon's own *Dawn*, which was being fitted with a new transom. On Hythe Quay shipwrights were just completing conversion work on *Northdown*; fitting new rails, bow and quarter badges. Also here were *Kitty* and *Centaur*. John Fairbrother was in the process of scarphing a new section into *Kitty's* transom. That day I counted fourteen barges alongside at Maldon, together with a trawler, a smack and Barry Pearce's former yawl *Ripple*: a forest of masts and spars set against the high stacks of Maldon's latest historic acquisitions—two steam tugs.

Until recently repair work on the tideway had been carried out at Norton's Yard in Bugsby's Hole. Dick Norton, with his assistant Fred (Plate 119), worked on many of the remaining trading and yacht barges. The workshop/office, which was a shed up against Redpath Brown's wall, was hung with old pieces of sail cloth, and in it was stored in seemingly no order whatsoever everything which could possibly be used for the repair of a barge's hull or her gear. Once, Dick's father and uncle had built barges here—*Scout*, *Serb* and *Scud*.

In the long, slightly shapeless hulls of the sprits'l barges there was more artistry in construction than is at first apparent, in shaping timbers to fit the gradual sheer of the hull, and in tucking the ends into the finely curved quarters and forefeet. While a modern yacht is delicately built under cover by a number of practiced men, few barges were accorded such facilities, and some were built under the

Plate 117. One of the sheds at the Maldon yards showing part of the collection of barge relics. (Picture the Author).

Plate 118. A leeboard being finished off at Cook's yard. (Picture the Author).

Plate 119. Familiar faces to bargemen . . . the team at the Bugsby's Hole Yard. Left: Dick Norton and right: Fred Bayly. (Picture Patricia O'Driscoll).

most crude of circumstances. It was common for a yard to be set up on any strip of waste land near the water, and "one-off" jobs were sometimes built on saltings alongside a convenient sea-wall, yet the hulls had to be solidly and lastingly built.

At a yard, building was carried out either by the owner or by his foreman. Dan's *Cecil Rhodes*, *Baden Powell* and *Uplees* were built by Edwin Anderson, the yard foreman, while Thompson built Smee's Maldoners. The master builder had the assistance of a master shipwright and each had an apprentice, although some did without. Timber was cut in an adjoining saw-pit, lengthwise, with the master working above and the apprentice below, keeping the saw steady and his eyes half-closed against the dust. Timbers for

the hull were of oak or pitch pine, laid single or double skin and rebated, fastened in former times with wooden "trunnels". Deck seams were filled and tapped home with the aid of a caulking chisel.

At first, early sprits'l barges were built in London, for by historical precedent the Thames was the birthplace of East Coast shipping; merchants traditionally finding greater profit in exporting their best timber to the London yards than to engage in local building themselves. In fact, certificates of ordnance for the 17th century showed that the majority of Eastcoasters were London built.

In time there were to be barge yards on almost every river between Great Yarmouth and the Kentish Stour. The greatest concentration was on the Medway and Swale, and in London, with Ipswich and Harwich trailing some numerical distance behind. Barge building at the smaller ports was slight. For example, although there had been a yard at Paglesham on the Roach since at least the early years of the 19th century, in one period of 27 years only six barges had been built there. The yard had been leased to William Kemp in the 1830's, whose son Alfred later laid down *Louisa* in 1855. But the cost of building *Paglesham* twenty-two years later proved too much, and Alfred went out of business.

Even at Maldon barge building tended to be occasional. Enthusiasts now remember John Howard's craft, of which *Violet*, *Sunbeam* and *Jachin*—which was rebuilt and renamed *Venta*—are afloat as housebarges, and *Ready* now renamed *Mirosa* which became a yacht and *Thoma II* which was built as one; but it must be remembered that Howard did not open his yard until the 1870's, and before that date only a handful of schooners and barges had been built in the port, among them *Beeleigh*, the little booms'l rigged *Tartar*, the rather famous *Rogue in Grain*, and Durden and James Williamson's hoys. Until Howard opened his yard local owners showed preference to patronise the Sittingbourne yards, which were well advanced in their design. James Keeble went there to commission *Eva Annie* and *Emily*, which were named after two of his three daughters; Strutt's early barges were built by Taylor at Murston, while Thompson's *Diligent* was built by Shrubsall.

Barges, however, were not only built on this part of the coast. *Mafeking* and *Adriatic* were built on the Humber, the Burham owned *July* at Boston in Lincs, *Thistle* and *Opal* were built in Scotland, and others were built at Rye, Lewes and Southampton. Inland, *Bertha* came from Bishop's Stortford; the steel ketch barge *Katherina* at Stadskanaal, while a number of Goldsmith's barges were built in Holland. The most far distant I am able to discover was Cardnell's German built *Fünf Gebruder* (Five Brothers) which began life far up the Leine at Hannover in 1842.

A century ago we would have found a number of different builders operating at any of the larger barge ports, some owning their own mast and blockmakers' shops, sited close to the rope walks and sail lofts. At Milton Creek barge building and its ancillary trades was a substantial local industry. Here, over 400 barges were built in the half-century from 1860, a third of them in one decade from 1860 to 1870, at least 25 being built in one year alone, 1866. In that half-century there were eleven separate barge builders. One of that number, Masters, was notedly erratic. Although he did for a while have a yard near Crown Quay he normally built anywhere he could find the space along the sea-wall. He used fruit tree wood and it is said that John Masters with the aid of a few apprentices took four years to build *J. D. Drake* on the wall near Churchfields. *Helvellyn* had been one of his earlier barges.

The building of cutter and sloop rigged barges at Crown Quay went back at least to the late 18th century. One of the earliest actual sprit-rigged barges to come from here was the *Hero* in 1811, which for 70 years maintained the Fairbrass hoy service to Whitstable.

James Matthams and George Peake were early builders here, and then in the 1860's the Crown Quay yard came into the hands of W. B. Spencelaugh whose *Thomas & Frances* lies hulked at Murston today.

The yard then passed to the Taylors. Stephen Taylor had formerly built at Murston, launching small river barges like the 43 ton *John & Edward*, but at Crown Quay he turned his hand to ketch and schooner rigged barges—*Thistle* and *Friendship* were two of these. Eventually, around 1898 Wills & Packham took over the yard. Their foreman at the time *Scotsman* and *C.I.V.* were built was a Mr. Masters. I wonder if this was the same John Masters whose

Plate 122. The Shrubsall built *Pall Mall* with Knight's *Our Boys* outside off Honduras Wharf in the 1890's. (Picture Author's Collection).

little yard, from which *Sarah & Eliza* came, was diagonally opposite on the sea-wall in Crown Quay Reach.

On leaving Crown Quay the Taylors moved to a site on the south side of Adelaide Dock. There was no permanent slipway here and if craft had to be blocked it was done by floating the blocks under a hull at high water. No barges were built here but a number of smacks were turned out. Tom Redshaw can remember his father going to collect the bawley *Providence* from Taylor's for delivery to Margate. Complete, her price was two hundred and fifty pounds.

Just round the bend from Crown Quay up on the east bank where the motor ballastmen now work to the ready mixed concrete depot was White's yard. Almost opposite this was one of the most prolific of the barge yards, that of R. M. Shrubsall. It is impossible to reckon with exactitude just how many barges Shrubsall did build but the number appears to be in excess of 50. Plate 122 shows his *Pall Mall* built in 1875, at the time of the photograph owned by Wakeley's and seen off their Honduras Wharf at Bankside with the

Plate 123. Cook & Woodward's Maldon yard, probably in 1896 when the frames were being set up, right foreground, for *Dawn's* building. Centre is the steam chest, known as the "coffin". From the crowds along the promenade it would appear to be a regatta day. Note, far right, how the promenade stops short by the mouth of the small creek, now filled in, which wound its way back to the foot of St. Mary's Church. (Picture the Author's "Dustbin Collection").

Rochester barge *Our Boys*, owned by Knight the Otterham brick-maker. Shrubsall was probably a descendant of the Mr Shrubsole whom we find was hoyman at Milton in the 1790's with the barge *Richard*.

Plates 46 and 149 give us some idea of what the creek looked like in those days. *Constance* is lying at Eastwood's Wharf which had been acquired after Shrubsall, while Lloyd's Wharf where *Yieldsted* is lying was up from Station Brickworks Dock. Above Lloyds was the old Milton tidemill.

There was a certain anonymity about barge building. A launching was often purely a local event. However exciting, it was so ordinary, especially at Milton that the people of those times found it un-necessary to record the occasion. Except for the occasional news-paper item few contemporary records were kept. For example at Rotherhithe in the 1760's, there were four mast and blockmakers, six sailmakers, two ropemakers and a number of boat builders. But even though some of the builders were well known, like Charles Hay's (whose firm was still flourishing under Robert Gray and Michael Paice over a century later), I am unable to fit the names of any of the Rotherhithe barges built before 1860 to their builders. At Faversham however, with the aid of the Georgian directories, I have had more success. I find in the 1820's and 1830's that Jos Pritchard was building at Standard Quay, probably employed as foreman to Redman, when *Harmony*, *Providence*, and *Commerce* were built. Then, William Chambers kept a mast and blockshop at Town Quay, near him George Crocker was practising as a sail-maker, and the hoy barges *Hope*, *Martha* and *Industry* had joined *Kent*, *Phoenix* and *Rochford* in maintaining the town's hoy service.

For the men at the yard, launching day was none the less conducted with great ceremony, and even if few written records survive, memories are still good and I own a number of excellent photographs which have been handed down through old bargeing families. The highest tide of the cycle would be chosen and work

Plate 125. *Olive May*, the largest wooden barge, at her launching from Wills & Packham's Crown Quay yard in 1920. (Picture by Courtesy of Alan Cordell).

Plate 126. *Raybel* at Wills & Packham's Wharf shortly after her completion. (Picture by Courtesy of Captain W. H. Hamilton).

at the port would cease for the event. Launches were not always simple affairs, as craft might be built some distance from the waterfront as at Swanscombe. At Halstow barges are remembered as having been launched diagonally across the dock, and at Goldfinch's Faversham yard a section of the wharf had first to be removed and a slipway constructed. In narrow creeks a launch might be made sideways as sometimes happened at Maldon Hythe.

Plate 123 shows the yard at the Hythe taken from the tower of St. Mary's Church in 1896. This particular photograph was found in a dustbin along with a number of others of the same vintage. The view shows *Dawn* over towards the pond being planked up, and to the immediate left of her hull is the steam chest which was known as the "coffin", near which the baulks of timber were laid for cutting in the saw pit. In front were the barge blocks—there appear to have been five in all—and when a barge was ready for launching a section of the wharf wall was removed and a slipway constructed, the barges being launched through the gap between the inner sets of blocks.

The Hythe lies at the foot of St. Mary's Church where the former seafarers' cottages fall higgledy-piggledy down to the waterfront. It is possibly the oldest quay in the town and is certainly the most attractive setting anywhere on the East Coast. It was a flourishing quay in 1516 when two new wharves and the town's "Coal Heape" were constructed. A contemporary plan shows there to be five wharves, a lime kiln and a chalk heap. There was also a dock,

Plate 127. Shipwrights at Goldsmith's yard, Grays, offering up a new port wale out of the steam chest. The barge is *Edith May*. (Picture by Barry Pearce).

Plate 128. The site of Smeed Dean's yard at Murston long after barges had ceased to be built there. Here most of the firm's barges were built and rebuilt. A lighter is up on the old blocks which were still in use until a few years ago by occasional craft. In the foreground lies the hull of the *Thomas & Frances*. (Picture Alan Cordell).

probably where the present yard is sited which appears to have been filled in around 1571 when the new wharf was leased to Robert Goddarde, Mariner, for a term of 40 years. The Quay was then owned by the Borough, although the annual rent of 16d. recorded in the accounts of the Borough Chamberlain for the lease of a quay and two shops to the Earl of Essex in 1536 hardly represents a fortune to the town.

Handley and Finch had had a boat building business here in the middle of the 19th century, then around 1890 the firm of Cook and Woodward was founded when James Arthur Woodward, who had served his apprenticeship as a shipbuilder under his uncle Mr Roote at Brightlingsea, went into partnership with his cousin, Walter Cook. There was a connection here with the Keeble family of barge owners for Walter Cook had married "old Ebenezer" Keeble's daughter. The actual building was performed by Woodward, who built *Dawn* in 1897, *Lord Roberts* in 1900 for Meeson of Battlesbridge, and *British King* for Hitchcock of Lavenham. But the partnership was dissolved in 1901, Cook continuing to repair barges, and now the yard is the most active repair yard on the coast.

For her launching from Wills & Packham's Crown Quay yard in 1920 *Olive May's* hull was bedecked with bunting. The ceremony was performed by Mrs Olive May Howton after whom the barge was named. A few years ago, before the barge was sold out of trade to be converted into a yacht, Mrs. Howton was invited to look over her by her skipper/owner Captain W. H. "Billy" Hamilton. *Olive May* was built for Mrs Howton's father, Captain Arthur Wenban, who formed Kent Coasters Ltd., and the barge has now been re-rigged with a standing-gaff (half sprit) mains'l.

Plate 126 shows another Wills & Packham built barge, *Raybel*, lying at Crown Quay in 1922, just after fitting out work on her had been completed.

Many trading firms had their own barge yards where a foreman was employed to build and repair. Some yards continued to be used until fairly recently. Plate 127 shows *Edith May*, then a motor barge, being fitted with a new port wale at Goldsmith's Grays yard in 1958.

With one of the largest fleet of sprits'l barges to maintain, Smeed Dean's yardmen had the task of repairing, lengthening and generally rebuilding that firm's barges. It is said that no Murston barge was considered to be beyond repair, however badly one might have been damaged. Around the turn of the century a sunken barge called *Lydia* was raised and refitted by them as the *Histed*. Smeed Dean also bought cheaply, raised and refitted several other wrecks including *Monitor* (which retained her name) and *Bexhill* which became the *Maid of Munster*.

In addition to buying cheap wrecks, Smeed Dean successfully raised and recommissioned several of their own unfortunate craft, including *Vincent*, *Donald*, which under Captain William Winn had foundered in the Estuary, and *Young Jack*. In fact, the firm rebuilt most of their own barges during the period 1903 to 1928, among them *Garfield* in 1920, *George Smeed* in 1922 and *Spurgeon*

Plate 129. Bill Raven the Maldon sailmaker splicing rope for a barge's mains'l in Taylor's sail loft. When the picture was taken in 1950 Bill had completed 59 years service in that loft. (Picture Conway Picture Library).

in 1924. In 1896, a Mr. Denham succeeded Mr Palmer as yard foreman, building the barges *Graham* and *Esther*, then re-building the then 95 year old *Favorite* in 1898, and re-building *George* in 1903. His workmanship was good for *Favorite* was to last for a further 70 years, becoming later a housebarge at Chiswick. His successor was Mr Orsford.

When they were rebuilt some barges were renamed. *Murston* had previously been the *Levetta*, and when Colonel Dean won the V.C. during the Great War, *Donald* was renamed *V.C.* in his honour. Other barges were shortened. *Sidwell*, named after Sidwell

Plate 130. Cecil Wright, then senior shipwright at Cook's yard, shaping down *Ethel Maud's* mainmast with an adze. (Picture Patricia O'Driscoll).

Plate 132. The stern of *Kitty*. Saddle chock, quarter board and part of the rail have been removed. The dark-coloured section of wood on the left of the letter "K" in the name has just been scarphed into the transom. (Picture the Author).

Plate 131. Tony Showell caulking a deckseam at Maldon aboard *Remercie*. (Picture Patricia O'Driscoll).

Drake, whose skipper for many years was the late "Bill" Kennett, was said to have sailed badly before her rebuild in 1922, but after a frame's length had been removed from her hull she was reputed to sail even worse than before.

Patricia O'Driscoll has recorded many aspects of repair and maintenance work on film. I have included some of these photographs to show caulking, splicing and shaping down spars, for there is always work to be done aboard: a deck seam required to be caulked, a length of rail has to be renewed and canvas that has to be patched.

When times were bad it was often not worth an owner's while to repair his barge decently, so leaks and rotten wood were not replaced but patched with concrete and filled with putty. This had foreshortened the lives of a certain number of barges. In time this poor workmanship makes itself manifest: the hull sags, frame heads rot, covering boards crack, and when nail sickness sets in it can often be the end of a barge. Every year one or two of them are stripped of their gear and towed off to a marshland berth to be burnt or to be left to decay.

Recently I came across a plaintive scrawl, possibly it had been penned by an unhappy mate, in the pages of a certain barge's log. The barge was obviously in need of urgent structural attention for the extract read "Not only does this barge leak from the bottom, she leaks from the top!"

Plate 133. Vic Forman, mate of *Vicunia*, **at work splicing a mooring wire. (Picture Patricia O'Driscoll).**

Plate 134. The orderly, uncluttered vista aloft. The heel of the sprit has been extended by the addition of a section of metal pipe. (Picture the Author).

Chapter VII
HULL, SPARS AND FITTINGS

To look at a sprits'l barge with her gear lowered away on deck you would be forgiven for wondering how her crew could possibly sort out what appears to be an irregular tangle of sails, spars, wires and cordage. Yet, once the gear is raised up again, the deck of a sailing barge takes on an orderly, uncluttered vista. Although designed for ease of handling, the arrangement of the gear viewed in isolation looks incredibly complicated.

The sprits'l rig is based on a diagonal spar known as the sprit which permanently supports the headrope of the mains'l. Traditionally this spar was of wood but now many barge owners have constructed metal sprits out of old trolley-bus standards; the rigged swim-headed lighter *Montreal* has one, and their advantage lies in

Plate 135. The arrangement of the mast-doubling. The heel of the topmast rests in the lower cap, and that mast is struck by being lowered on the topmast heel wire (seen in between the topmast and mainmast doubling). First the heel wire takes the strain of the mast then the fid which rests over the edges of the capping is removed from the heel. When loading or alongside another craft the crosstrees are topped by means of the crosstrees lifts. (Picture the Author).

the great saving of weight. The mainmast rests in a tabernacle on deck which allows the gear to be lowered away, either to pass under bridges or to allow the gear to be serviced. First the topmast is lowered and then the mainmast and sprit is lowered by means of the stayfall tackle which connects the forestay with the stem-head. The wire stayfall is lead from the stayfall blocks and wound round the barrel of the windlass. Plate 136 shows the blocks with the wire coiled over the windlass bitts in readiness to lower away. At one time these blocks were of wood, and forestay and stayfall of hemp: Plate 28 shows the massive arrangement on an old time stumpy barge. Traditionally the stayfall wire is taken in three turns around the barrel and led back over the starboard bitt head to be surged away once the stopper on the wire has been removed. The stayfall is then surged out until the hounds of the mainmast lie just over the after hatch coaming, when a mast prop is inserted. By this method the gear is jerked down and, to avoid putting this heavy strain on the windlass and bitts, some prefer to wind the entire wire around the barrel, take off the pawls of the windlass and then wind the gear down. It takes strong men to do this. It could be a dangerous exercise if the run is too great, and is a very non-professional practice.

Lowering, fitting and raising the gear up is a tricky business and even with care brails are sometimes rigged wrongly and in heaving

Plate 136. A centre pawl windlass. The end of the stayfall tackle is coiled over the starboard bitts in readiness to lower away. For'ard of the windlass the heel of the bowsprit rests in a tabernacle. (Picture the Author).

Plate 137. Stems of the coasters *Ardwina* (left) and *Lady Gwynfred* (right). Compare the iron stayfall blocks with the wood ones on the *Alfred*. (Picture the Author).

up, vangs can catch under the corners of the coamings or in the mizzen rigging. Personally I have never enjoyed lowering away, for on two occasions I have witnessed a mast come down in a hurry. The first time I had just gone aft to remove the mast prop. The stayfall took the weight, the wire jammed in the blocks and snapped. On the second occasion the stemband parted. Both were rather unpleasant experiences.

Once a year when in trade a barge would go up on to the yard where her gear was lowered and overhauled, and the sails taken ashore to be mended and dressed. Today, barge yachts usually unrig at the end of the season, store their sails for the winter and dress them in the early springtime. It is a messy job.

First a convenient spot has to be found, sufficiently large to lay out around 1,300 to 1,500 square feet of mains'l. At Maldon this is done in front of Taylor's sail loft where the grass seems permanently tinted an unusual shade of "ochre-green", while one crew had a preference for a certain tennis court—I wonder if the players noticed the smell. The ingredients and the actual mixture are said to be closely guarded by those who purvey sail dressing, but basically it comprises a large quantity of sea water which is placed in a mixing container and to which cod oil is added followed by red and yellow ochre in that order, which when applied to the sail with brooms smells not too unpleasant but has a natural ability

Plate 138. *Pretoria* at Union Wharf, East Greenwich, with her gear lowered . . . an irregular tangle of sails, spars, wires and cordage. (Picture Patricia O'Driscoll).

Plate 139. The difference in hull design between, left centre, the river barge *Westmoreland*, and centre *Edith May*. Note the pronounced sheer of *Edith May*. (Picture the Author).

Plate 140. The arrangement of winches aboard *Lady Gwynfred* where a single drum winch is used in addition to the three-barrel winch, seen on the left. (Picture the Author).

to rub off onto anything the sail may come in contact with.

Freshly dressed, sails are folded or wound into sausages to be hoisted aboard and if you are lying "second bottom" your neighbour will not love you much for dragging your tacky sails across his hatches. The mains'l is then laid out along the mainmast with the headrope over the sprit end, overhanging the stern, and with the body wormed under the mast ready to be shackled to the jackstay. Plate 138 shows *Pretoria* with her gear lowered away. The mains'l has been removed already and the mate is unlashing the tops'l from its hoops.

Captain Fred Cooper produced "A Handbook of Sailing Barges" some 18 years ago which excellently illustrates the way in which rigging is set up, and most bargemen find it helpful to refer to this work.

It is not until you see two barges of differing sizes alongside each other that you realise how much more powerful the hull of a coaster looks in comparison to, for example, a river barge; as in Plate 139 where *Westmoreland* is lying alongside *Edith May*. On deck Patricia O'Driscoll is seen chatting to the late Jack Spitty. With their finer underwater lines and higher bows some of the coasters were awkward to handle light-laden as their bows presented a high area of windage. Deep-laden, however, they scored, for while the river barges often ploughed through seas the coaster would ride them.

Sailing performance was a matter of balance, of hull, rigging, leeboards and rudder. Some skippers continually toyed with the set of their rigging in order to achieve maximum speed. Even a small alteration in the set could improve a barge's handling. It was one of Brice's barges which had a reputation for sailing badly. A new skipper took over, inserted a small wedge between the heel of the mast and the mast-case and then raked the topmast for'ard until the truck was over the centre of the fore hatch. Performance was greatly improved.

The heavier gear of a coasting barge is not easily hand-handled and some of these barges came to be fitted with additional winches. The single-drum main brail winch was always sited on the port side of the mast case, but if a three-barrel winch was used, the tops'l and fores'l halyards were taken to the two outside drums, with the main brail taken to the lower drum. Some barges carried two winches. The middle and lower brails were taken to cleats on the port side of the mast case, visible in Plate 140. Compare the arrangement of winches in this plate of *Lady Gwynfred* with those of *Westmoreland* in Plate 142.

On either quarter are crab winches used for lowering and raising the leeboards. The cast iron winch is a relatively modern innovation in barge history. Up until the latter years of the 19th century most barges were fitted with tackles. Crab winches when they were introduced were either of a perpendicular or arched type, see Plate 143, and both incorporated warping drums on the outside, but many Faversham and Milton craft were fitted with capstans instead. The lower drum, fitted with a pawl, held the leeboard wire, while the upper was used for warping, as seen in Plate 144 of *Iota*.

Plate 141. Gardiner's improved three-barrel brail winches. (Picture by Courtesy of Alan Cordell).

Plate 142. A single drum main brail winch aboard *Westmoreland*. (Picture the Author).

Plate 143. A perpendicular shaped leeboard winch known as a "Combine"
crab winch. Note that this type of
winch has a single spindle in place of
the more usual two, which was pushed
in to engage the centre drum if the
outer drum was to be used for warping.
(Picture Patricia O'Driscoll).

Plate 144. A capstan winch aboard
Iota. To lower the leeboard the pawl
was taken off the lower drum and the
wire was allowed to run out. It was
often checked by the timely placing of
a boot on the lower rim. (Picture
Patricia O'Driscoll).

With this method a bolt had to be dropped in to connect the lower drum, but otherwise the warping drum was free to revolve. Having an all-round lead for warping was an advantage, but this was offset by there being no pawl to the upper drum. The set of capstans aboard *Ironsides* came from the *John & Mary*.

In the days when sprits'l barges were fitted with leeboard tackles tiller steering was the order of the day, and little mizzen sails were balanced on masts fitted to the port sides of the rudder heads. An unusual adaptation of this rig is seen in Plate 145 where the stack barge carries a standing lug mizzen. The first wheel-steered barges were equipped with chain steering. The arrangement of this gear with the more modern worm and screw steering may be seen by comparing Plate 146 of *Ida* with Plate 147 of Cremer's *Edith*. When barges were tiller steered earlier examples were still to be found which had fine, tucked-up quarters and high cabin tops, with a water barrel lashed on chocks to the port side of the cabin top.

Plate 145. A lug mizzen in place of the more common sprit mizzen aboard an old-time stack barge off Honduras Wharf. Note the high-peaked sprit and flat tops'l. (Picture Walter F. Dowsett Collection).

Plate 146. The chain steering arrangement aboard *Ida*. The advantage of this system was that if a barge sat in a bad berth where her rudder was forced up the steering mechanism would not be damaged. The worm and screw system was especially vulnerable. (Picture Patricia O'Driscoll).

Plate 147. The worm and screw steering aboard *Edith*. The rudder box has been removed. If the spindle was damaged, as happened once to *Ernest Piper* the rudder could not be handled. With chain steering a low, wide rudder box was fitted. (Picture Patricia O'Driscoll).

Plate 148. The small water breaker which many barges carried on deck. This was taken ashore in the barge boat to be filled up at every opportunity in order to keep the main tank full. (Picture Patricia O'Driscoll).

Chapter VIII

PORTRAITS IN SAIL

There is something strangely majestic about any ship which has become a derelict—and many famous vessels have ended their days in this way. I am, quite frankly, fascinated by them. I find ship remains lying by the edge of the marshlands; neglected, their exploits, passages and the very men who sailed in them have become forgotten—almost as if these things had never happened—yet with some people it is a natural instinct to want to picture what such craft were like, when the plankless decks were spruce and painted up, and when the mud and grass-filled cabins were well-panelled homes. Always I want to know more about them.

Largely through the efforts of Joe Hines, Tom Redshaw and Alan Cordell, there is now a concise list detailing nearly all the barge remains around the coast, together with a potted history of their respective lives afloat, from the remains of the *May Queen* and *Gleaner* at Wainfleet Haven to the wreck of the *Four Sisters* in the Menai Straits. However, before this register was compiled, finding out the name of a particular barge was often a matter of scrabbling around in the mud attempting to uncover lettering on the transom or bow rail which might yield a name and port of registry or, if they were not intact, tracing the official number carved on the main beam. If the barge enthusiast is fortunate, information of this nature could be gleaned from local men who perhaps remembered the barge being placed where she was, in a number of cases over 40 years ago. Sometimes I meet people who had familiar knowledge of some of these craft and have kept old photographs of them, yellowed at the edges from having been carried around in a pocket book for a half century. Charlie Kirby gave me one. He took it with the box camera he had found among a freight of rough-stuff loaded aboard *E.F.Q.*, back in about 1923. Photographs for this book have come to me in that way.

Near Kingsferry Bridge on the Swale there used to be the remains of two barges, *Livingstone* and *Yieldsted*. Here, it proved not too difficult to trace *Yieldsted's* history afloat as Alan Cordell's Grandfather, Captain James "Jim" Fenteman, had been master of her some 85 years before and Alan has been able to unearth a series of photographs of the barge. She was built at Rochester in 1870, probably as a stumpy, being rebuilt at Sittingbourne by Shrubsall 29 years later.

Yieldsted carried more sheer than was normally to be found in river barges of her day; this is noticeable in Plate 149 taken by

Rammell, the Sittingbourne photographer, while at Lloyd's Wharf just after her rebuilding in 1899. She is carrying the reduced sail plan worn by all the "brickies" for winter work in the Estuary. Black, brown and green bands adorned her sprit. She was unusual among barges in that she carried up until 1910 a vane instead of a bob at her topmast truck, which depicted the Rampant Horse of Kent. When Mr Andrews purchased a half-share in the barge she exchanged her vane for the blue and white striped bob worn by all privately-owned barges which worked for Smeed Dean, including *Favorite*. It is now worn by the *Lord Roberts*.

Yieldsted was built originally for Joseph Alexander of Holling-

Plate 149. Rammell's study of *Yieldsted* at Lloyd's Wharf in 1899. Note the vane at the topmast truck and the unusually shaped stem. Only two shrouds are carried either side. (Picture Alan Cordell Collection).

Plate 150. *Yieldsted* at Gransden's Wharf in 1905. (Picture Alan Cordell Collection).

Plate 151. Captain James Fenteman in 1909. (Picture Alan Cordell).

bourne, being named after one of the nearby downland villages. It was around 1887 that Jim Fenteman became master of her. The first sprits'l barge Jim joined was the *Georgiana*, one of his early freights being 3,000 bushels of sprats from Brightlingsea to Murston, for use as manure on the Smeed farms.

Later, in *Yieldsted*, Jim carried bricks and cement out of Milton Creek returning with ashes or rough-stuff, with the occasional freight of coal for the gasworks. It was sometime during the 1890's that he became part owner of the barge, and was appointed managing owner for the syndicate which acquired her. His principal partners were Mr Matson and Mr Gransden (of the local brick-

Plate 152. Montague Clarke's painting of *Yieldsted*. (Picture reproduced by Alan Cordell).

Plate 153. Remains of the *Yieldsted* at old Kingsferry bridge in November 1957. The new bridge now has a raising centre section which is fitted to allow barge yachts passage through. It is a speedy and very efficient process. (Picture by Alan Cordell).

making firm of that name) and so *Yieldsted* came to be employed in carrying bricks away from Gransden's Wharf. Plate 150 shows her lying alongside that wharf in Crown Quay Reach in 1905; the building partly obscured by the barge's brailed mains'l is Wills & Packham's shed. When the barge came to be rebuilt Alan discovered that Captain Fenteman had been forced to sell his house to pay for his share of the bill, but being a shrewd man, had put the residue of the sale money down as a deposit on a new house.

When Matson died the syndicate broke up. Jim extended his interest to half the shares and the other half was purchased by Mr Andrews of Smeed Dean's and from then on that barge worked to the company's Murston wharves. But before then in 1903 ill health forced him ashore and he became harbour master at the Creek in 1912, a position he was to hold for 19 years, while still retaining managing ownership of *Yieldsted*. As there was not enough work to keep him fully employed in this official capacity he also took on the job of managing Murrell's Wharf and later became a director of the Kent Barge Owners' Association until they were dissolved in 1923. Part of his duties was the examination of masters.

For a while Jim's eldest son was mate with him on *Yieldsted* but he left the barge around 1902 to become a fireman with the London Fire Brigade. One of the members of the brigade was Charles Montague Clarke, a well known artist, who in 1905 was persuaded to make an oil painting of *Yieldsted*. It is reproduced in this book. Later Clarke painted a second and smaller work of the barge for Captain Fenteman himself.

After Captain Fenteman left the barge a series of skippers were employed to sail her, among them the noted "Scranny Jack" Hambrook who achieved fame aboard her during the great gale of December 1914 when a number of local barges including *Lydia*, were lost. *Yieldsted* was lying to her cable off Canvey Island when the gale struck and as the batten bar to the fo'c'sle scuttleway was missing "Scranny Jack" stood on the scuttle throughout the gale to prevent its washing off and the seas from filling the barge.

The end of her trading career came during the slump of the 1930's when there was a serious fire in her after cabin at a time when she was lying on Cremer's Berth, below Murston. The barge sustained considerable damage. As it was not thought worthwhile to repair her the hull was sold to Dick Evenden, the Kingsferry huffler, who cut the damaged part of her transom out and used the barge as a floating dock for the small craft which he used to repair. She was in use as such until 1938 then gradually began to decay, Dick taking timbers off her hull as and when he required a supply of firewood for his stove. Twenty years later *Yieldsted* was found to be lying in the path of the proposed new Kingsferry Bridge and her remains were broken up.

With other barges one is not so fortunate in being able to trace details of their histories. Some of the hulks around the coast cannot even be identified by the more elderly bargemen. Such is the case of a set of barge remains at Maylandsea, and also one in Althorne Creek near the *Nell Gwyn*. If a barge is converted into a housebarge

Plate 154. A three-masted schooner at Murston gas works in 1905. Note the long, peaked bowsprit, and the sheer size of the schooner in comparison with the sprits'l barges behind. (Picture Alan Cordell Collection).

her new owners may change the name into something quite un-nautical. This in time may make identification nearly impossible. I have no idea who *Annabelle* might have been—but she was possibly named after some society "bird" for the barge was moored at Cheyne Walk and broken up a few years ago. I watched her remains being burnt from Alan Chidgey's *Raven* moored across the river at Swan Dock. It took nearly a week. As for *Annabelle's* former neighbour *Tish*—I can only suggest that her name was a rather rude anagram!

In Captain Fenteman's day fore-and-afters were common in Milton Creek, bringing coal to the Murston gasworks, but more numerous were the ketch barges. One of them, *Hydrogen*, had been built as a tank barge by Gill at Rochester and was later bought by Smeed Dean. The late Edgar March acquired a rare photograph of her, now in the possession of Walter Dowsett, showing the barge setting an incredible sail plan: four headsails were carried, fores'l, two bowsprit jibs, a long topmast spinnaker, and to balance them a mizzen tops'l was set. Smeed Dean converted her to a "mulie" rigged barge.

When the Smeed Dean fleet broke up in the 1930's and many of the barges passed into the ownership of the "Combine", *Hydrogen* was acquired by Andrews. An 88h.p. auxiliary Kelvin was fitted in 1941 when she came to be owned by Sully's, and during the last war the barge served in Scottish waters. For *Hydrogen* this was a return to familiar territory, for in her early years she used to work occasionally to Grangemouth. Now she is one of the few remaining wooden motor barges in trade. Plate 156 shows her under motor at Great Yarmouth.

Down at Seasalter on the East Swale buried quite deep in the mud near the Sportsman public house is the remains of the old Maldoner *James and Harriet*. The outline of her frames is visible at low water and in the evening when the sun is going down it casts long, low shadows from her hull along the wide mudflats.

The barge was built round-bowed at Maldon in 1864, and an account of the launching expected that she would be a fast barge. Her owner was William Smee, coal and timber merchant, and she was named after two of his children. Smee had wharves just below Fullbridge, and in his day owned one of the largest fleets of barges on the Blackwater, comprising the swimmie *William &*

Rebecca, Morning Star, Thomas, William & Lucy, which replaced the original St. Osyth built schooner of that name, *Surprise, Three Sisters*, the Sandwich-built schooner *Surprise*, the Maldon built schooners *Emily* (1863) and *Maldon* (1862), the brig *Scotscraig* and the brigantine *Daring*. Later his craft were looked after by his son, James, while another son, George, was manager of J. C. Carter's fore-and-afters like *Robert Adamson* which worked out of Heybridge Basin. When William died *Scotscraig* was sold to Carter.

James & Harriet worked with the fleet mainly in the timber trade, but she appears to have done some grain work with the occasional freight of coal from the Humber. On Smee's death she was sold to John Howard, around 1880 passing to John Sadd, and finally ending her days under Holland at Whitstable in the 1930's. Her last skipper at Maldon was George Hales, now in his mid nineties, while another Maldon man who commanded her was Charles "Pup" Simmons.

"Pup" first sailed on the collier ketches bringing coal to Heybridge Basin in 1864. *James & Harriet* was "Pup's" last barge; he went master of her in 1915 and retired in 1922 at the age of 70. Previous to her, on leaving the ketches, he had gone into Strutt's barges, *Two Friends, Three Sisters*, and *Ann Elizabeth*, of which his son, also called Charles, was master around 1909, before taking Prior's *Jesse* in 1910. The origin of the nickname appears to be lost, but

Plate 155. Crundall's *Savoy* was built at Rochester to carry stone for the rebuilding of Dover's piers. (Picture Douglas West Collection).

Plate 156. *Hydrogen.* (Picture the Author).

"Pup's" sons who were masters of *William & Richard*, *Tit Bits*, and *Pall Mall* respectively were known as "Charlie Pup", "Tom Pup", "Jack Pup", and a fourth as "Bill Pup". Even today "Pup's" grandson is still known by the delightful nickname of "Charlie Pup's Son"! He too followed in the family tradition, and was master of the Howard-built *Jess*, later cut down in Harwich Harbour.

Strutt's barges were sailed three-handed, "Pup's" sons and later his grandsons, starting as boys with him at the age of 11. The pay was 2/6d. per week for the boys although the masters and mates were paid by shares. There was no allowance for a slow

Plate 157. Remains of *James & Harriet* **in the East Swale. When the sun is going down it casts long, low shadows from her hull along the wide mudflats. (Picture Alan Cordell).**

passage, and during the bad winter of 1895, "Charlie Pup" once took six weeks to get from London to Maldon, presumably in the *William & Lucy* which was trading to Lasts at Heybridge with chalk for lime making. The weather was so cold and still and the ice was so thick that the barge could not move at times. Plates 160 and 161 show *Russell* and the tiller-steered lighter *Peter* of Lambeth, caught in the ice during this terrible winter.

Unexpectedly some barges took on a completely new lease of life after their working days were over. 15 years ago I am sure few could have imagined that some of the former sprits'l barges which had been stripped of their gear and were then used for lightering

timber into Heybridge Basin would ever be re-rigged for sailing.

It was the late John Otter, however, who bought the *William Cleverly* as she lay in the Basin, just a bare hull with no gear or fittings, newly retired from her lightering duties, traced her up the Navigation, moored her to the bank and began to re-rig her—the first time, I think, that this exercise had been performed privately from a bare hull. On limited capital, John acquired every single item of rigging and deck fitting from between 30 and 40 other barges.

Sidney "Bill" Blake was appointed master, and with mastcase fitted and mainmast aboard, *William Cleverly* was towed out to a berth along the sea-wall in Colliers' Reach close to Tom Saunt's old tug, which in 1946 had towed her round from the Medway to become a lighter. New sections of decking, rails and lining were fitted; knees were shaped up; "Dilbury" Clark made a pair of oak horse-chocks; while an unknown stonemason made the barge a gift of magnificently carved transom boards, "*William Cleverly, Rochester*". A pair of leeboards was acquired at Maldon and made up into a raft with 40-gallon oil drums lashed alongside to be floated down round Herring Point behind a motor boat. The sails were lashed up into sausages and carried along the track from the Basin over the heads of the picnickers sunning themselves at Whitsuntide under the lee of the sea-wall.

Gradually the barge took shape, the sails were bent on and the gear was ready to be raised (Plate 164). Soon, only the tops'l had to be repaired and the leeboards bent on. It was unfortunate that *William Cleverly* was never to sail. I had gone out to Hong Kong at the end of the summer, and shortly afterwards I received a telegram to say that John had died suddenly. The barge was sold, her gear went into *Ethel Maud* and *William Cleverly* became an unrigged barge in Colliers' Reach. In John's memory, we gave a trophy to the Blackwater Sailing Barge Match.

I had always imagined that the barge had been named after William Cleverley, the Ipswich marine artist, with a mis-spelling of his name, but Eric Watt has suggested to me that she might have been named after the William Cleverly who was a shipbuilder, responsible for building Navy ships at Gravesend from about 1790. Among them was the 64 gun *Director* of which Bligh was Captain during the Nore Mutiny of 1797. The barge herself was built by the Co-operative Barge Building Society at Borstal in 1899 for A. E. Horsenail, the Strood corn factor. Later, she passed to the London & Rochester Barge Company, and in the last war was requisitioned for powder storage in the Medway Creeks.

William Cleverly was not a typical river barge even though she was only 46 tons. She was finely built with more sheer than is customary on the Medway barges, with a graceful, shallow transom and narrow bow. She was fast and undoubtedly wet! Victor West, son of the noted "Schoolmaster" West went master of her in the 1920's when she was trading all over the Kent, Essex and Suffolk coasts, taking up to 500 quarters of wheat to Ipswich and sea-walling with ragstone to such places as Shelford Head on the Maplin Sands. The ragstone was loaded at Milhall, near Maidstone, and Victor West, who later became master of the petrol tanker, *Stourgate*, took a series of photographs of her being loaded there. "Sea-walling" provided an independent life for the crews engaged in this work.

Bill Blake recalled how, in Wakeley's *Estelle*, he had loaded rag-stone at Point Chute above Tovil footbridge, or at Allington where he sometimes loaded stone dust for Deptford Creek (where it was used for making asphalt). Bill remembers that at Point Chute, barges went on to the berth headfirst, being moored to the trees. Here trucks were run down a runway, and their loads were tipped 20 feet into the barge holds. No wonder that barges in this trade were so knocked about.

On leaving the Medway, Bill would set off "down Swin" towards the Blackwater or Brightlingsea Creek where a green flag would be displayed on the sea-wall at the point where the cargo was to be discharged. Once at Thames Haven he was forced to be stern on to the sea-wall. In these exposed positions the barges lay-to, with an anchor out to seaward, and sometimes they were blown up the wall.

It was a lively life at times, especially in *Estelle*, which was so flat-shaped that when she lay at anchor once under the West Shore, off Sheerness in a breeze, the sea came over the bow and went off aft. "She had almost as much freeboard for'ard and aft as she did amidships," Bill ruefully remembers!

The London home of Wakeley's barges was Honduras Wharf on Bankside, and near here also was Albion Wharf where Cunis's barges berthed. Edward Perry remembers that the crews used to meet in the bar of the Founder's Arms (I wonder if it was named after the nearby Hoptons Charity). It was around here that he got to know many of the London River sailormen, including Jack Huggy, who Edward believed was the last of the local hufflers. He recalls that one day he went down to Bankside where Huggy was getting Goldsmith's *Yampa* ready for sea. The skipper and mate were in the broker's office so Huggy moved the barge out into mid stream. He cast off, "and then, with a strong spring tide running

and quite a bit of wind, he got her out into the fairway and made her fast to the buoy. All done single-handed without fuss or bother."

It was Huggy who drew Edward's attention to one of Wakeley's barges which was nick-named the "Ghost Train" after the stage thriller of the 1930's. The barge was *Lurline*, formerly owned by Clement Parker at Bradwell, and she received her nick-name from her skipper, a taciturn, hard-working chap, who had no time to go near the Founder's Arms, and was concerned only with getting unloaded and away for another cargo. He brought her in laden with sand regardless of holidays, bad weather, strikes or any other obstacle to cargo carrying.

Plate 161. The lighter *Peter* trapped during the great frost. Note the hand-spike windlass for'ard which was a feature in all early barges. The lighter in Plate 28, has a similar windlass, and the one on *Alfred* is just discernible. (Picture by Courtesy of the Executors of the Late E. P. Olney).

Plate 162. *Westmoreland* trapped in the frost at Lower Halstow during January 1963. (Picture Alan Cordell).

Edward has made a particular study of how barges got their names and some were quite imaginative. The old swim-header *Clyte* which used to tie up below Blackfriars, usually with a cargo of rubble, was named perhaps with a twist of humour after a water nymph; many of Covington's craft were named after literary characters, *Sam Weller* and *Pickwick* for example, and the reason for this naming, he was told by the Skipper of *Chieftain*, was that "the Guv'nor was fond of reading!" Although *Speranza* had a name which was the Italian word for hope, she was in fact a sad barge. It was while moored on Starvation Buoys at Woolwich that there was a fight between the skipper and the mate, during which the former was stabbed to death.

The foreman at Willment's Wharf, Bankside, was a chap named Paddy, and although he handled dozens of barges each week he only went afloat on one occasion, and that was when he was persuaded to take a trip down to the Mud Hole behind a tug. But Paddy did not like the idea of having nothing to hang onto in a craft only fifteen inches from the water, and when the barge arrived off the Prospect of Whitby he could not wait to get ashore fast enough. 15 inches . . . he was lucky!

Plate 163. *William Cleverly* in the Chelmer & Blackwater Navigation in 1961, as she was when she finished her lighterage duties. The first few precious blocks have been assembled on her hatches. (Picture the Author).

Plate 164. *William Cleverly* two years later alongside the sea-wall in Colliers' Reach, so named after the colliers which were too deep drafted to reach Maldon, and so used to anchor here and discharge into lighters. Mainmast and sprit have been hoisted aboard and the deadeyes are about to be rove. Aft, part of the mains'l is stretched out for repair. (Picture Patricia O'Driscoll).

Chapter IX
THE END OF AN ERA?

The decline in the fortunes of the sprits'l barge as a trading medium began in the early 1920's and, of course, it was heightened during the depression when so many barges were laid-up for want of a freight. The centuries old pattern of trade had perceptably begun to change, the handling techniques of consignees no longer required bulk cargoes to be carried by sail. Tugs with lighters, small steam and motor powered coasters were sometimes more economic to run than sailing barges; on the land road locomotives were able to haul heavy loads long distances. Most significant of all was the advent of the motor lorry which had proved its prowess during the war. The age of the lorry was to be more forceful in its upheaval than ever the steam railway had been, its effects more damaging.

The decline was most evident in Kent where the barges relied heavily on the building material trades for their freights, and where owners had embarked on programmes of rationalising their interests, amalgamating and weeding out their smaller and older units. The demand now was for larger freights, carried outside the Estuary, work for which many craft were unsuited. A limited number of barges were still being built, at East Greenwich, Maidstone, Rochester, Sittingbourne and Mistley: *Wilfred*, *Marie May*, *Lady Jean*, *Phoenician*, and *Adieu* were some of the ones to be built at these ports respectively during the 1920's, and some owners like Arthur Wenban made brave attempts to form small but specialised firms, while a number tried to make a living as skipper/owners, carrying cereals, feeds, scrap metals, petrol, timber, coal and gravel. An attempt was even made to revive the hoy trade by a group of Margate businessmen. The hoy work had come to an end at Faversham around 1900 and at Margate in 1915 when service with the *John Bayly* ceased, but the Margate men in 1924 acquired a motor barge in which Tom Redshaw's father went mate. Eventually it came to be realised that there was little future in sail by all but a few owners.

The number of barges to be owned at Faversham halved in the ten years after the Great War, from a fleet of 30 craft, which included the coasters *Beryl* and *Aubrey*, and one of the last ketch-barges to keep her sails, *Goldfinch*. On the Blackwater there had been 56 barges in 1916, so Donald Wright has calculated, but by 1933 only 17 remained, and on the Crouch and Roach there were only 6.

The Maldon craft had been reliant on the stack trade so that

Plate 165. On board *Venta* in 1963 shortly before his death, John Otter with his back to the camera is seen chatting to Bill Blake, who is explaining how a "featherbed" gybe is controlled. (Picture the Author).

Plate 166. Almost rigged and ready for sea. Only the leeboards, which are out of sight for'ard, the quarter boards and the mizzen remain to be fitted. At the time of the photograph the tops'l was ashore being finished off. Shortly after this *William Cleverly's* sails were re-set for the first, and almost the last time. (Picture the Author).

when horse transport went out of fashion the market for hay and straw and the supply of muck-outs for the land had become meagre. Stacks were still worked right up until the middle of the 1930's on the Crouch and Blackwater but in very decreasing numbers so that the Maldoners were forced to look for other trades. Many turned to bringing "London Mixture" for the local farms and "Tubby" Blake did a lot of this work in *Southwark* and *Fanny*, visiting almost every landing in these waters. He frequently traded to Millhead and to the now dammed Lion Creek where he used to keep a small yacht, near to where *Neepawa* was broken-up.

Some of the older stack barges were unrigged during this period. Keeble's old *William & Arthur* and *George Cookson* became timber lighters for Woodcroft and Clark at Heybridge Basin. Roger Minter has recorded that *Albion* ceased to trade. *Percy* went to Ipswich owners and *British King*, flagship of the "Blue Bobbed Fleet" was sold to Sully's for £1,100. At Battlesbridge, Meeson-owned only *Roache*, *Paglesham* and the small barge *Rainbow*, the *Rettendon* having gone to Rochester owners just before the war. Soon *Roache* was to go, and when the family sold the mill to Matthews the last two barges were disposed of.

At Colchester however, the barge fleet was being expanded by Josh Francis who had bought Howe's barges at auction in 1921, and then taken over managing ownership of the Keeble fleet. Gradually Francis drew many of the then remaining Essex barges into his partnership, and the firm of Francis & Gilders Ltd., was formed on 2nd October, 1933. As fresh barges were acquired the older units joined Woodcroft and Clark's lighterage fleet. *Unity* was one of the first, being booms'l rigged for the timber work, and *Diligent* followed around 1930, although she remained fully rigged for a few years. *Peace*, *Keeble* and *Malvina* were others. But elsewhere in Essex the barge fleets were still being reduced. In 1933, the year after Clement Parker died, there were only three of his

Plate 167. *William Cleverly* at sea around 1926. (Photograph, the Late Captain V. West).

former barges *Invicta*, *Victa* and *Plantagenet* left at Bradwell.

After the depression was over and when the economics of the country improved there were fewer men available to make their livings under sail. It was no longer worth the while to repair the older barges whose condition had deteriorated after being laid-up, and when some of them were put back into trade it was with auxiliaries that they were fitted. Those less fortunate were patched, not repaired, and it was cheaper to do this with concrete than with wood.

To some barges the Second World War proved to be a new lease of life, even if it was only for lighterage duties, and *Diligent*, which had been unrigged in 1935 and might soon have been expected to be broken-up, was dispatched for duty in Harwich harbour. Others which were serviceable went back to sea. Many of the Kentish river barges which had been laid up in the Swale and Medway creeks at the outbreak of war were requisitioned for powder-storage and balloon barge work. From those who recall such days it was an uneasy life for the crews of these craft, a lonely and dangerous one too, anchored in the creeks. It was *Kingfisher* which was badly damaged and lost her stern when a German aircraft was shot down and crashed on her. Her hull was taken to Stangate Creek where she still lies today. For one reason or another others were lost: *E.F.Q.* sank off Sheerness in December 1944, *York* sank in Sharfleet Creek, the *Hereford*, *Dundonald*, *Wiltshire*, the London & Rochester Trading Company's *Carlotta*, *Gladys*, and *Godwit* were also casualties.

The barges in sailing commission played a very valuable part in the war, especially during the early years, when sailing craft were among the few able to move easily between London and Ipswich, in spite of the efforts by the Royal Navy to hamper their movements! In the exposed channels of the Estuary mouth the barge was especially vulnerable to either attack from enemy aircraft or from mines.

Plate 169. One of the last freights of cement to be worked under sail, the "ironpot" *Cambria* in Saltpan Reach, while under the ownership of the L.R.T.Co. in May 1950. (Picture Alan Cordell).

Plate 168. "Sea-walling". The Kent Rivers Catchment Board's *Llandudno* under tow at Strood in the late 1940's. Alongside her is a lighter used by the Board. (Picture Author's Collection).

Perhaps I have painted a depressing picture, and in many ways it was, yet barges still found cargoes and there were strong fleets at Colchester, Ipswich, Rochester and at London. Both owners and crews took a great pride in their vessels which were smartly painted and well maintained where possible, and it was this high standard of maintenance which enabled them to continue trading at all. Nevertheless so many of the barges which had been in commission in 1939 were never to work again after the war. Many of these had been requisitioned and in 1946 the high cost of putting them back into sailing condition would have been prohibitive, for others there was just no work. Some became motor barges, others

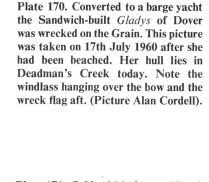

Plate 170. Converted to a barge yacht the Sandwich-built *Gladys* of Dover was wrecked on the Grain. This picture was taken on 17th July 1960 after she had been beached. Her hull lies in Deadman's Creek today. Note the windlass hanging over the bow and the wreck flag aft. (Picture Alan Cordell).

Plate 171. Goldsmith's former "iron' pots" ending their days as timber lighters for Sadd's at Maldon in the mid 1950's, *Scotia*, *Briton*, *Scot*. Among the wooden barges used for lightering here were the Curel built *Agnes & Constance*, *Leslie West* (now a housebarge for Richard Duke at Pin Mill), *Beaumont Belle* (which is now hulked in Heybridge Creek), *Oak*, *Teresa*, *Cecelia*, and the lighters *Grange* and *Cypress* which had been built at Maldon and although the Registers show them to have once been sprit-rigged this cannot be remembered. After being raised *Emma* ended her days here, and after the war her remains were towed into Heybridge Creek, where they joined those of many other craft including *Falcon*, *The Sisters*, and the collier schooner *Merton*, which dated from 1819. (Picture the Author).

housebarges or yachts, or were just hulked. *Kappa*, *Coot*, *Mid Kent* and *Curlew* were just four of those which, on their return, were sold and then broken up at Otterham, their remains later being burnt. *Lapwing* was one of a number to be hulked in Stangate Creek. I was looking at her remains only the other day: she would have made an ideal yacht, but then who could have anticipated that 20 years hence there was to be such a revival of interest in barges.

Some which became yachts enjoyed a longer lease of life and a few receive more attention than a number of their former owners could have afforded to give them. It was mainly the smaller barges which became yachts at first, for their larger sisters were making good money in the post-war boom. *Iota*, *Gold Belt*, and *John & Mary* were three which were converted to barge yachts shortly after the war. In the case of Cremer's *John & Mary*, she was laid up on the foreshore at Whitstable in 1946, one of four of that fleet to be converted around that time, as there was then a serious shortage of crews at Faversham, only four men to man the four remaining barges. *John & Mary* (J. & M. as she was known), was purchased by Squadron Leader D. H. "Nobby" Clarke who was able to replace her gear only by acquiring items from other laid-up barges.

Soon there were all but a handful of barges trading without

Plate 172. *May* **running dart before the wind in one of the Medway Matches. (Picture the Author).**

Plate 173. *May*, left, and *Spinaway C.*, locking out of the K.G.V. entrance, 3rd August 1958. (Picture Lawrence Mahoney).

Plate 174. *Westmoreland* coming up to Hollow Shore. The fores'l has been dropped in readiness to wind, and Colin Frake has come alongside in his motor boat to give her a pluck up.

Plate 175. *Portlight* at Crown Quay in 1956 to unload a freight of canned tomato juice. (Picture Alan Cordell).

Plate 176. *Xylonite* about to pass under Rochester Bridge on her way up with wood pulp for New Hythe. (Picture Patricia O'Driscoll).

Plate 177. *Repertor* at Mistley after conversion. The wheelhouse was built up above her cabin top. Note the form of chain steering and the iron rudder. When the original engine was installed the crew's accommodation was moved for'ard. A metal barge sweats and because of this we found it necessary to keep an oil stove alight in the accommodation the whole time we were aboard. A rather large scuttleway formed the entrance to the foc's'le, and this protruberance was known at Mistley as the "telephone kiosk" (see Plate 100), and the fores'l had to be lowered and lifted over this scuttleway before the barge went about, as it was too high to allow clearance of the sail. (Picture the Author).

auxiliaries and even yacht barges were becoming rare through ultimate neglect. In the early 1950's Goldsmith's fleet was disbanded, the remaining craft being sold to the L.R.T.Co. Some of their former iron-pots continued sailing until around 1952 when most of them were sold for scrap, *Kismet, Geisha, Yarana* and *Astrild* being broken up at Bloor's Wharf, Rainham, where they joined *Lorna* which had been unrigged after incurring severe damage in 1951. One of the last, the iron-pot *Cambria*, is shown in Plate 169 in Saltpan Reach in 1950, working a freight of cement. *Scotia, Scot* and *Briton* were sold to Sadd's at Maldon to become unrigged timber lighters; they are shown tied up in Heybridge

Creek in 1956 in Plate 171, while *Trojan* became a motor barge.

Surprisingly, there were cargoes to keep a modest fleet under sail in the 1950's. At Ipswich the sailormen were *Memory, May, Venture, Spinaway C, Anglia* and *Marjorie;* on the Stour, Horlocks kept their three steel-built Mistleymen *Portlight* which took an unusual freight of canned tomato juice to Crown Quay in 1956 (Plate 175), *Xylonite*, and *Repertor* which was soon fitted out as a tops'l auxiliary and would have been better off without an engine, as we found out! Everard's owned *Cambria*; Plate 97 shows her in the river, and they kept *Sara*, and *Veronica* for racing, later acquiring *Dreadnought* from I.C.I. The L.R.T.Co.'s *Sirdar* and Eastwood's *Westmoreland* were also kept for racing purposes only. The muster was completed with I.C.I.'s eight powder barges and Daniel's Whitstable-owned *Colonia* which was to sink in the Swale in October 1956. There were also a number of fine tops'l auxiliaries most of them in the coasting trade. Shrubsall's *Veravia* often worked

Plate 178. *Victoria* leaving Milton Creek 23rd April 1949. By then Ellis' *Maria*, *Pimlico* and *Victoria* were the only working sailormen to remain at Sittingbourne, and shortly afterwards all three barges were disposed of, leaving just the motor barges *Charles Burley*, *Ninety Nine*, *Mildreda*, and *Pride of Sheppey*. (Picture Alan Cordell).

Plate 179. The auxiliary *Dawn* passing Greenwich. Her master at the time was Peter Powell. The wheelhouse section could be removed to enable the barge to pass under the low bridges leading to Colchester's East Mills. (Picture the Late W. H. "Bill" Kemp).

"down Channel" as did the L.R.T.Co.'s *Alan*, *Pudge*, *George & Eliza*, *Thyra*, *Scone*, *Cabby* and *Marie May* and Everard's *Will Everard*. Paul's owned *Tollesbury* and *Thalatta*, Horlock's *Remercie*, Francis & Gilders' the *Alaric*, *Dawn*, *Varuna* and *Lady Helen*, Daniels' the *Savoy*, and finally there were the 2 Essex mill barges *Ethel Maud* and *Leofleda*.

Trade for them was both varied and interesting. There was wheat to Ramsgate, coal from the Humber, wheat and cattle cake to Great Yarmouth, paper for Norwich, wheat for Beccles, stone from Dean Quarries loaded under the chute inside the Manacles Rocks in Falmouth's bay, which was surely one of the most uncomfortable

Plate 180. The motor barge *Thistle*, one of two barges to be built in Scotland loading "inside" a ship in the docks. In this position a barge could sometimes be crushed against the quay. (Picture C. Beazley).

Plate 181. The motor barge *Wyvenhoe*, one of 3 iron sailing barges built at Wivenhoe. Alongside her is the iron barge-type coaster *Maloney*. (Picture C. Beazley).

berths on the coast, and cereals, timber, fertilisers for Colchester, Maldon, Stambridge, Mistley, Ipswich, Rochester, Faversham and Whitstable. *Thyra* made passages to the Humber and up the Nene to Peterborough, *Veravia* and the motor barge *Convoy* worked occasionally to the Channel Islands while *Will Everard* was seen almost everywhere from Cornwall to the Humber. In 1955 as an auxiliary she was in trouble off Dungeness while on passage from the Isle of Wight to King's Lynn, and was towed into Dieppe, while in the same year *Pudge*, now owned by the Thames Barge Sailing Club, grounded off the Lincolnshire coast, and was towed to Grimsby.

Plate 182. Barge racing in the 'seventies. *May* and *Remercie* lead *Redoubtable* and *Vigilant* up the London river in the Greenwich Festival Barge Match, June 1973. (Picture by Martin Treadway).

This then was the history of trade by sailing barge for by the early 1960's only *Cambria*, the *May*, the *Venture*, and the *Spinaway C* remained, they, a handful of auxiliaries and a number of motor barges. It was the end of an era. Correspondents sadly predicted that within one or two years the lofty topmasts and canted sprits of the sprits'l barges would be just a memory.

But they were to be proved wrong, for the young men who joined as mates in the ten years after the war and came to command some of the last barges to trade without engines seemed determined to keep sail alive in one fashion or another. There was no future in attempting to continue trading, although the Thames Barge

Plate 183. The revival of post-war barge matches . . . traffic congestion before the start of one of the Pin Mill matches, left *Dawn*, rear centre *Venture*. Photographed from *Lady Gwynfred*. (Picture the Author).

Plate 184. An idle seascape, perhaps an artist's dream but a bargeman's nightmare, as without steerage way on the tide collisions can occur. Here *Edith May* under command of Jack Spitty creeps past *Lady Gwynfred*. (Picture the Author).

Plate 185. *Ironsides* knuckling-down after being re-rigged. Since then she has been fitted with a larger suit of sails, a longer sprit, and her rails have been painted a conventional black. (Picture B. Tillman).

Preservation Trust's *Memory* had made a brave effort some years before, and there wasn't exactly much money in owning a private barge yacht, but there was money in chartering to fee-paying passengers. Not enough perhaps to make a profit, but enough to keep a barge in commission, and it was this which gave the impetus for the revival of interest in sprits'l barges. John Fairbrother and Barry Pearce were two former barge skippers who took timber lighters from the unrigged fleet at Heybridge Basin to re-rig them as barge yachts for the passenger charter trade. Now instead of taking cereals to Colchester or Ipswich they take charterers to Brightlingsea.

Plate 186. Determined to keep sail alive in one fashion or another. John Fairbrother's **Kitty** has been rigged with a bowsprit and in light airs sports a mizzen stays'l. On the Medway a class for bowsprit barges has now been revived. (Picture the Author).

In 1962, when it was planned that the next year's Centenary Thames Match would be the last, 2 local barge matches were started up, one at Pin Mill, the other on the Blackwater. The local matches proved such a success that now there are 7 of them. At Faversham we have organised our own combined match with classes for barges and oyster smacks; there is a similar event on the Colne, and a new Thames Match on the tideway.

Of the barges which compete in these matches some have been re-rigged from motor barge or lighter hulls, their owners completing major restoration jobs which a few years ago would not have been considered worthwhile. Alan Reekie, for example, bought the iron motor barge *Ironsides* when she was about to be sold for scrap. She was a single hatch barge with no mastdeck by then, and I am sure nobody thought to see her sailing again, but Alan cut out a section of her hatch, welded in a mastdeck, acquired *Wolsey's* gear and a suit of sails. Even a serious fire which below decks almost gutted *Ironsides* from end to end, burning out the hatch-coamings, proved to be not too serious a setback, for new coamings and hatches were fitted and the interior was redesigned. Recently a very pleasant sail aboard her shows that she handles perfectly.

Every year a number of motor barge hulls are restored and re-rigged, though perhaps an equal number of older barges are taken out of commission. It can cost now from £5,000 to £6,000 to buy a barge hull with engine straight out of trade, on top of this they then have to be fitted out, while the reservoir of hulls capable of conversion is obviously diminishing. At the time of writing Cranfield's former *Kimberley*, Sully's former *Beatrice Maud*, of which Harold Smy had been master for many years, are undergoing restoration. Another former Cranfield barge which had sunk after being in collision in the Thames was *Orinoco*. After lying first at Greenhithe and then in Oare Creek her present owner, Lawrie Tester, is rigging her out again. The problems of fitting-out are highlighted when one realises that *Orinoco's* new sprit was ordered as a baulk of timber in Canada, brought over to Tilbury and then shipped by lighter to Faversham Creek.

For some years now, well-informed students of sail have predicted that the era of the sprits'l barge had not long to run, and that this span of life would be determined not only by the craft themselves, but by the availability of men to sail and care for them. Somehow they just continue, even though it is difficult to acquire replacement gear and to find suitable moorings. The barges which sail today do not have to experience the all-the-year-round conditions they formerly had to in trade; their owners are able to maintain them well, while there are patient men who have the time to teach young enthusiasts something of the hereditary skills which were passed down to them. Up and down the coast skilled men are going back into history to learn how some of the older jobs and crafts were done. Now there is this new lease of life in the hands of private owners I think there is a reasonable chance that with careful handling we might still see barges competing in matches for many years to come, and some of the hulls afloat today might

Plate 187. The enthusiasm for the sprits'l barge, and indeed for other former working boats, is enormous ... here a barge and a Colchester registered smack pass off Elmley Island. (Picture the Author).

Plate 188. In the 1950's a number of motor barges were laid up in and around the Swale ... *Glenbury*, *Nelson*, *C.I.V.*, and *Dee* at Queenborough. Subsequently *C.I.V.* was re-rigged and *Dee* became a housebarge. (Picture Patricia O'Driscoll).

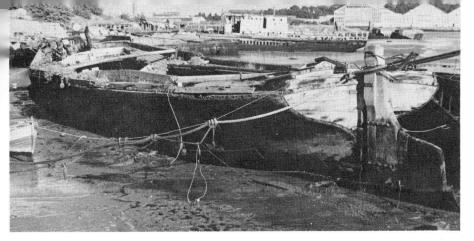

Plate 189. Old barges take a long time to die. . . . Many were hulked after service in trade, or as roads barges or housebarges, and some were broken-up at Whitewall Creek on the Medway. Here Eastwood's former brick barge *Bedford* is gradually being stripped away. (Picture, in 1962, by Alan Cordell).

Plate 190. Other barges were towed into position alongside sea-walls, their bodies eventually sink into the mud or marsh and grass grows through their hatchways. Here, left to right, are *Meteor*, *Violet*, *Metropolis*, *Henry Wood*, *Bessie Hart*, and foreground *Partridge* from which this photograph was taken. At the now dammed Lion Creek near Paglesham is the remains of the ketch *Providence* through which an elder tree is growing, while in a silted-up creek near Gunpowder Dock on the Swale there is a sunken harbour of old barges. Some of them have been there for 40 years, buried up to their decks. One hull is almost completely intact and after digging down the number on her main beam could be read. It was of a barge *Hope* which disappeared from the Registers in the 1860's, but it is possible she became used for Government service. Another is the old *Princess Royal*. (Picture, in 1957, by Alan Cordell).

Plate 191. Old frayed wires, cleats, deadeyes and blocks — all buried in the mud. All that history. . . . The remains of the barge *Ninety* at Frindsbury. (Picture Patricia O'Driscoll).

see the century out. Then, craft like *Cabby* will be only 72 years of age, younger than some of today's barges.

The enthusiasm for the sprits'l barge is enormous. The Thames Barge Sailing Club has over 500 members, while the Society for Spritsail Barge Research has over 100, and both these bodies publish their own Journals which are valuable contributions to barge history. The members of this latter body founded the Dolphin Sailing Barge and Museum Trust at the site of a former barge building yard on Milton Creek. But the keen interest extends to beyond the actual restoration and sailing of barges. We are now becoming conscious of our changing environment and we are

Plate 192. Dusk in Brightlingsea Creek. (Picture Alan Cordell).

Plate 193. Patterns on the sea *Centaur* **of Harwich. (Picture**

Plate 194. Grey tints inlaying every colour in the seascape . . . Arthur Bennett's *Henry*. (Picture Les Arnold).

Plate 195. Spars bowed, perfectly balanced, chine almost awash . . . *May*. (Picture Les Arnold).

anxious to uncover local history. Many perhaps are also prompted by the knowledge that the barge is a symbol of a period which lies only just around the corner in man's memory, and find her a suitable link with which to connect the present and the past. If the sprits'l barge prompts people to take notice of the sea and its habits, of the shore, of wildlife and landscapes, and above all of values then this is perhaps what bargeing is all about.

The tide mills (except for the one at Woodbridge), the steam-powered saw mills, the locomotives, the traction engines and the paddleships, the lime kilns and the carts and the broughams have gone. So, too, have some of the elegant, Georgian, stucco-faced

Plate 196. A sight we might not see again . . . *May* with gear lowered lies to a buoy off Blackfriars after delivering Portland stone for the restoration of St. Paul's Cathedral. The stone blocks lie in the foreground, and the dockers broke their strike for the afternoon to unload the cargo. (Picture the Author).

Plate 197. Smeed Dean's *Youngarth*, named after Garth Doubleday, off the Murston gas works shortly after her building. (Picture by Courtesy of Alan Cordell).

houses, the weather boarded cottages and the mellow wharfside buildings. We may not care for it but some people call it progress. Many of the barges mentioned in this book also have been lost or broken up. You will find some of their remains scattered on the edge of the marshlands which fringe the Thames Estuary, on the Swale, Medway, Crouch and Blackwater, or lying against wharves in places which are not ports any longer. There is not much left of the greater number of these derelicts, just old timbers, the stump end of frames, rusty spikes, old frayed wires, cleats, deadeyes and blocks—all buried in the mud. All that history. . . .

Plate 198. Smeed Dean's *Maid of Munster* **ex** *Bexhill,* **seen here as the** *Bexhill,* **up above bridges during the early years of the century. (Picture by Courtesy of the Executors of the Late E. P. Olney).**

Plate 199. A stack barge off Tower Bridge at the turn of the century waiting to pass through to the Upper Pool. (Picture Walter F. Dowsett Collection).

Addendum. *Westmoreland* sank at Hoo in late August 1973. Her hull, declared a Constructive Total Loss, now lies beached at Hoo. A decision has yet to be taken whether her hull could or should be rebuilt.

Dick Norton of Bugsby's Hole died in September 1973.

Bibliography

The reader will probably be familiar with many of the books written on sprits'l barges so I feel there is no need to provide a list of these. Instead I will mention some of the other books which I have consulted for my references.

For details of the craft themselves I have used the Mercantile Navy List and Maritime Directory, but I would caution readers that these lists do contain a great number of errors. For example, *S.D.* is listed as being ketch-rigged, yet old bargemen remember her well as being a barquentine barge, while *Lady Gwynfred* is listed as being of only 8 Registered Tons! For the details of the hoys and earlier passage craft, and for the descriptions of the various ports I have turned to some of the following: The Universal British Directory (1798); Johnstone's London Commercial Guide and Directory (1810's to 1820's); Robson's Home Counties Directories (1830's); Pigot's various Directories (1820's to 1840's); Wright's History of Essex (1848); and the Conveyance sections of the Post Office Directories (1840's to 1900's). For pilotage and coastal descriptions I commend the New Seamen's Guide and Coasters Companion—my own copy is dated 1806—read in conjunction with Admiral Knight's charts.

For details of agricultural practice and freights Arthur Young's County volumes on the General View(s) of Agriculture are very concise, while the statistician will be interested in H. Rider Haggard's Rural England, which is a useful guide to wages paid. Thomas Kitson's Excursions in the County of Essex contains some valuable descriptions of the coastal towns.

For a description of the brickmaking industry Frank G. Willmott's Bricks and Brickies (1972), with photographs collected by my colleague, Alan Cordell, is a delightful book.

There have been countless volumes written on London River, but I would just mention three of them: Tomlinson's London River (1921), and Linney's two volumes; while for knowledge of inland waterways I commend Peter Smith's recently published Waterways Heritage. Although nothing to do with barges whatsoever one of the finest books on East Anglian life is W. A. Dutt's The Norfolk Broads (1903), which contains some of Southgate's wonderful illustrations of wildlife and wherries. Articles on Sprits'l barges appear regularly in the East Coast Digest, and the journals of the Society for Spritsail Barge Research and the Thames Barge Sailing Club.

RHP

Register of remains of former sprits'l barges to be found around the coast

The Register includes only craft which appear to be derelict or have been broken up. Many of them have substantially deteriorated and only the occasional floor timbers remain of some.

Extracted from the detailed Register and maps compiled by members of the Society For Spritsail Barge Research, 1973.

Wainfleet Haven (Lincs):	*May Queen* of Rochester, *Gleaner* of London.
Scott Head, Brancaster Island:	*H. Brouncker* of Rochester.
Barton Broad, Norfolk:	*Federation* (possibly renamed).
Southwold, Suffolk:	*Martin Luther* of Rochester.
Orford, Suffolk:	*Tuesday* of Rochester, *K.C.* of London.
River Deben, Suffolk:	*Dover Castle* of London, *Three Sisters* of Maldon.
Dovercourt:	*Edwin* of Rochester, *Mary Ann* of Harwich, *Emily* of London.
Parkeston:	*Pride of the Stour* of Harwich.
Shotley Gate:	*Inflexible* of Ipswich.
Felixstowe:	*Alaska* of Rochester, *Landfield* of London.
Ipswich:	*Sextus* of Harwich, *Excelsior* of Maldon, *Audrey* of Ipswich.
Pin Mill (Orwell):	*Challenger* of Rochester, *D'Arcy* of Maldon, *Charles Hutson* of Rochester, *Florence* of Harwich, *Jess* of Maldon, *Daisy* of London, *Anna Maria* of Faversham.
Woolverstone (Orwell):	*Emily* of Ipswich, *Theresa* of London.
Levington Creek:	*Castanet* of London.
Mistley:	*Edinburgh* of Rochester, *Anthony* of London, *Gravelines II* of Ipswich.
Hamford Waters:	All craft now said to have been broken up.
Brightlingsea:	*Joseph* of Rochester, *Kardomah* of Rochester.
St. Osyth:	*Bluebell* of Rochester.
Fingringhoe Creek:	*Fly* of London.
Beeleigh:	*George & Annie* of Rochester.
Fullbridge (Maldon):	*Lord Roberts* of London, *Diligent* of Maldon, *Golden Hope* ex *G.A.M.C.* of Rochester.
Heybridge Creek:	*Grange* (Lighter), *Cypress* (Lighter), *Spray* (Lighter), *Merton* (Schooner), *Sisters* of Maldon, *Falcon* of Maldon, *Agnes & Constance* of Rochester, *Emma* of Maldon, *Black Eagle* of Rochester.
Opposite Maldon Quay:	*Keeble* of Maldon, *Excelsior* of Harwich, *Emily* of Ipswich.
Maldon Promenade:	*Lancashire* of London, *British Lion* of Rochester, *William Cleverly* of Rochester.

Northey Island:	*Gilman* of Rochester, *Mistley* of Ipswich.
Saltcote Creek:	*Betsey* of London.
Goldhanger Creek:	*Snowdrop* of Harwich.
Tollesbury:	*Hyacinth* of Maldon.
Mersea Strood:	*Unity* of Ipswich, *Fanny* of Maldon, *Victa* ex & *Co.* of London.
Maylandsea:	*Hawk* of Rochester, *Hannah* (probably renamed).
Wallasea Island (Crouch):	*Neepawa* of Rochester, *Mundon* of Maldon, *Argosy* of Rochester, *Harry* of London, *Scarboro* of Rochester, *Landrail* of Rochester.
Burnham:	*George.*
Stow Creek (Crouch):	*Cerf* of Rochester, *George Cookson* of London.
North Fambridge:	*William & Arthur* of Maldon.
Wakering:	*Duke of Kent* of Rochester, *Gazelle* of Maldon (remains lie on shore).
Millhead:	*Pride of the Orwell* of Ipswich.
Leigh Creek:	*Eva Annie* of Maldon, *Welsh Girl* of Rochester, *Eureka* of Harwich, *Diligent* of Faversham.
Benfleet Creek:	*Henry* of Rochester.
Holehaven Creek:	*Southwark* of London.
Grays:	*Brave* of London, *Lilian* of Rochester.
Erith:	*Edwin* of Rochester, *Percy* of Harwich, *Orient* of London, *Redshank* of London.
Blackwall Point:	*Royal George* of Ramsgate, *Iverna* of Harwich, *Hilda* of Ipswich.
Cliffe Marshes:	*Anna Maria* of London, *Coombdale* ex *Triumph* of London.
Northfleet:	*Garfield* of Rochester, *Dunstable* ex *R.G.H.* of Rochester.
Swanscombe:	*John Byford* of London, *Windward* of Rochester.
Isle of Grain:	*Renown* of Maldon, *Alfred Little* of Rochester.
Halling:	*Alice* of Rochester.
Cuxton:	*Albion* of Maldon, *Daren*, *Pride of Ipswich*.
Borstal:	*Ebenezer* of Rochester, *Five Sisters* of London?
Strood, Pelican/Temple Marsh:	*Curlew* of London, *Irex* of Rochester, *Imperial* of London, *Maysie* of London, *John Evelyn* of London, *London Belle* of London, *Godwit* of Rochester, *New Trader* of Rochester, *Sam Weller* of London, *Dabchick* of London, *Bethel* of Rochester, *Sidwell* of Rochester.
Strood:	*Grace* of Ipswich, *Harry*, *Jim Wigley* of Rochester, *Redwing* of Rochester, *Ninety* of Rochester, *Ariel* of Rochester, *Mollie* of Rochester, *Azima* of Rochester, *Gipsy* of Rochester.
Rochester:	*Margery Alice* of Rochester, *Cygnet* of London, *Sphere* of Rochester.
Chatham:	*Ethel Margetts* of Rochester.
Gillingham:	*Lizzie* of London.
Whitewall Creek:	*Una* of Harwich, *Berwick* of London, *Holborough* of Rochester, *Milton* of Rochester, *Arthur Relf* of London, *Aline* of Harwich, *Rathmona* of Rochester, *Bedford* of London, *Squawk* of Rochester, *Rutland* of London, *Norseman* of London, *Duplicate* of London, *U.V.W.* of Rochester, *Shamrock* of London, *East Anglia* of Rochester, *Bittern* of London, *Scout* of London.
Hoo:	*Violet* of Rochester, *G.C.B.* of Rochester, *Mildreda* of London, *Freston Tower* of Ipswich, *Metropolis* of Rochester, *Northumberland* of London, *Henry Wood* of Rochester, *Meteor* of Rochester, *Pioneer* of Faversham, *Partridge* of Rochester, *Bessie Hart* of Faversham.

Stoke Saltings:	The remains of all the 12 barges here have been completely disintegrated.
Otterham:	(All craft burnt to floors). *George* of Rochester, *Bessie Taylor* of Rochester, *Curlew* of London, *Heron* of Rochester, *Kappa* of London, *Coot* of London, *Gamma* of London, *Mid Kent* of London, *Alpha* of London, *Saucy Kent* of London, *Sigma* of London, *Plover* of London, *Theta* of London, *Kentish Maid* of Rochester, *Irex* of Harwich, *Rand* of Rochester, *Kent* of Rochester, *Sirdar* of Ipswich.
Rainham:	*Frederick & Mary Ann* of Rochester, *Scud* of London, *J.E.G.* of Rochester, *Dundonald* of Rochester, *Bobs* of Rochester, *Dick Turpin* of Rochester.
Lower Halstow:	*Ernest & Ada* of London, *Devon* of London, *Surrey* of London, *Whaup* of London, *O.L.S.* of London, *George & Ellen* of Rochester, *Durham* of London, *Harold* of London.
Stangate Creek:	*Carlotta* of Rochester, *Eva* of Rochester, *Kingfisher* of Rochester, *Dorothy* of Rochester, *York* of London, *Gladys* of Rochester, *Emily* (ex W.D.), *Hereford* of London, *Wiltshire* of London, *Lapwing* of London, *E.F.Q.* of London.
Funton Creek:	*Squeak* ex *Dorcas* of Dover.
Shepherd's Creek:	*Viola* of Rochester, *Gladys* of Dover, *Teetotaler* of Rochester, *Ella* of Faversham, *Maria* of Rochester, *Meridian* of London, *Admiral Blake*, *Ernest Piper* of London.
Queenborough River:	*Victory* of Faversham, *Nelson* of London.
Queenborough Creek:	*Northampton* of London, *Baden Powell* of Faversham, *Surprise* of Colchester.
Milton Creek, Head:	*Vera* of Rochester, *Protector* of London, *Pioneer* of London, *Stanley* of London, *New Hope* of Maldon, *Emma & Sarah* of Rochester, *Dauntless* of Rochester.
Crown Quay Reach:	*Dorothy* of Harwich, *Arcades* ex *Olive Mary* of London, *Klondyke* of London, *Fanny Maria* of Rochester.
Fronting Adelaide Dock:	*Nashenden* of Rochester, *Monkwood* of Rochester, *Pheonix* of London, *Donald A.* of London, *Wye* of Rochester, *Loualf* of Rochester, *Alliance* of Rochester, *Jessie* of Rochester, plus other remains.
Ballast Wall Reach:	*Harmony* of Rochester, *Strathmore* of Rochester, *Nesta* of Rochester, *Excelsior* of Faversham.
Churchfields Wharf:	*Scud* of London, *Genesta* of London, *Carisbrook Castle* of London, *Ventura* of Rochester, *May* of Rochester, *Pomona* of Rochester, *W.B.* of Rochester, *Edith* of Rochester, *Our Boys* of Rochester, *Lizzie* of Faversham, *Vectis* of London, *Sidney* of Rochester, *Sportsman* of London, *Ninety-Nine* of Rochester, *Baltic* of London.
Murston:	*Thomas & Francis* of Rochester, *Gladstone* of Rochester.
Elmley Ferry:	*Mersey* of Rochester.
Elmley Island:	*Webster*.
Conyer:	*Landrail* of London, *George* of Rochester, *Gore Court* of Rochester, *June* of Rochester, *Bessie* of Rochester, *Dabchick* of London, *Band of Hope* of Rochester, *Kestrel* of London, *Nonpariel* of Rochester, *J.M.W.* of London, *Thomas & Arthur* of Rochester.

Uplees:	*Economy* of Faversham, *Maltster* of Rochester, *Samuel Bowly* of Rochester, *Pride* of Sandwich, *Princess Royal* of London, *Hope*.
Oare Creek:	*First Attempt* of Rochester.
Harty Ferry:	*Corona* of London, *Lizard* of London, *New World* of Rochester.
Windmill Creek (Sheppey):	*Sheppey* of Rochester.
Rye Harbour:	*Orient*.
Newhaven:	*Federation* of Colchester, *Albert* ex *Ada Mary* of Rochester.
Piddinghoe:	*Thetis* of London.
Littlehampton:	*Jane Mead* of Rochester.
Velder Creek (Langstone Harbour):	*Zebrina* of Faversham, *Camber* ex *Belmont* of Faversham, *Justice* of Harwich, plus a number of local barges.
Weymouth:	*Bessier* ex *Bessie* of Rochester.
Bridgewater, I.o.W.:	*Crowpill* ex *John Wesley* of Cowes.
Bembridge, I.o.W.:	*Gwalia* ex *New Zealand* ex *Four Brothers* of London, *R.B.* of Rochester, *Blackwater* of London.
West Cowes:	*Eloc* ex *Bessie*, *Louisa* of London, *Lucretia* of Ipswich, *Richmond* of Rochester, *Gerald* of Rochester, *Grebe* of Rochester.
Tewkesbury:	*Monarch* of Sittingbourne.
Menai Straits (Moleydon):	*Four Sisters* of Faversham.

Note: This Register cannot be guaranteed accurate at time of publication as, since it was compiled, some remains may have been dispersed. There are also a number of unidentified remains which have not been included herein.

Index and register of craft mentioned

Name	Registered	Built		Tons	Remarks	Page
Blessing					17th Century hoy	32
Brenda	Faversham		P.E.I. (1879)	225	Brigantine	28
Britannia	Faversham	Goldfinch	Faversham (1865)	42		36,45
British King	Maldon	Cook & Woodward	Maldon (1901)	59		78,106,135
Briton	London	Fay	Southampton (1898)	80		77,137,140
Burnham	Maldon	Shrubsall	Sittingbourne (1864)	42		38
Cabby	Rochester	Gill	Frindsbury (1928)	79		142,148
Cambria	London	Fay	Southampton (1899)	66		30,136,140
Cambria	London	Everard	Greenhithe (1906)	79		28,40,73,76
						140,144
Carlotta	Rochester		Rochester (1892)	44		136
Cecelia	London	White	Sittingbourne (1903)	80		137
Cecil Rhodes	Faversham	Dan	Faversham (1899)	49		77,98
Centaur	Harwich	Cann	Harwich (1895)	60		21,28,48,97
						148
Challenge	Weymouth		Ipswich (1899)	70	Sank 1925	78,80
Champion	Maldon		Rochester (1865)	44		50
Charles Burley	London	Burley	Sittingbourne (1902)	52		141
Charlotte	Maldon		Limehouse (1799)	41		83
Chieftain	London		London (1893)	59	Sank 1945	132
City of London	London		Nine Elms (1825)	41		36
C.I.V.	London	Wills & Packham	Crown Quay (1901)	46		101,146
Clipper	Rochester	Watson	Rochester (1875)	42		86
Clytie	Rochester		Limehouse (1878)	46		132
Colonia	Harwich	Felton	Sandwich (1897)	62	Sank 30.10.1956	140
Columbus	Faversham		Sittingbourne (1868)	36		88,93
Commerce	Faversham	Redman	Faversham (1825)	36		103
Company	Rochester		Sittingbourne (1897)	45		79
Connaught	Rochester		Nine Elms (1879)	38	Rebuilt 1905	50
Constance	Rochester		Sittingbourne (1879)	40		36,46,103
Constant Trader	Yarmouth		Yarmouth (1788)	110	Hoy	34
Convoy	Dover	Smith	Rye (1900)	73		11,143
Coombdale			(1887)	65	ex *Triumph*, Rebuilt Greenwich	87
Coot	London	Letley	Halstow (1894)	36		138
Crouch	Maldon	Kemp	Paglesham (1867)	50		92
Curlew	London	Letley	Halstow (1897)	44		138
Cypress	Maldon		Maldon (1887)	44	Lighter	137
& Co					See *Victa*	
Daring	Maldon		Sunderland (1846)	166	Brig	125
Davenport	Ipswich		Ipswich (1877)	72		26
Dawn	Maldon	Cook & Woodward	Maldon (1897)	54		97,102,103,104
						106,141,142,144
Dee	Rochester	White	Sittingbourne (1898)	46		146
Delta	London	Springett	Maidstone (1898)	41	Sank 1944	55
Derby	Rochester	Smeed Dean	Murston (1878)	32		64
Diligent	Maldon	Shrubsall	Sittingbourne (1877)	45		100,135,136
Donald					See *V.C.*	
Dreadnought	London	White	Sittingbourne (1907)	70		140
Dundonald	Rochester		Rochester (1897)	50	Ex *Mabel Maud*	136
Dunstable	Rochester	Smeed Dean	Sittingbourne (1891)	49	Ex *R.G.H.*	51
Durham	London	White	Conyer (1899)	42		87

Name	Registered	Built	Tons	Remarks	Page
Dyamund				17 Century hoy	32
Edith	Rochester	White Sittingbourne (1904)	48		44,52,54,58
					72,82,117,118
Edith May	Harwich	Cann Harwich (1906)	64	Named after Edith May Cann	40,47,68
					69,74,105,106
					114,144
Edward	Rochester	Strood (1857)	41		93
Edward	Faversham	Sittingbourne (1881)	45		43
E.F.Q.	London	Letley Halstow (1900)	32	Named after Ernest Frederick Quilter	75,119,136
Elizabeth	Maldon	Maidstone (1841)	64		47
Elizabeth & Mary	Maldon	Sittingbourne (1870)	44		38
Ellen	Maldon	Sunderland (1860)	91	Ketch	82,83,84
Emily	Maldon	Northfleet (1844)	32		84
Emily	Maldon	Thompson Maldon (1863)	93	Schooner	125
Emily	Maldon	Ipswich (1869)	85		47
Emily	London then Maldon	Sittingbourne (1883)	45		38,100
Emily Lloyd	Maldon	Taylor Sittingbourne (1872)	126	Ex *William Levett*	27
Emily Smeed	Newhaven	Smeed Dean Murston (1872)	272		27
Emma	Maldon	Howard Maldon (1897)	64	Became lighter, 1941	137
Emma Mizzen	Rochester	Rochester (1886)	50	Sank	40
Endeavour				Hoy barge	92
Enterprise	Yarmouth	Bessie & Palmer Southtown (1891)	168		47
Ernest Piper	London	Piper Greenwich (1898)	65		118
Estelle	Rochester	Rye (1899)	44	Roads barge 1947	129
Esther	Maldon	Sittingbourne (1863)	44		39,56
Esther	Faversham	White Faversham (1900)	43		42,52,64
Esther	Rochester	Smeed Dean Murston (1900)	50 then 62	Wrecked off Ramsgate	77,108
Ethel	Faversham	White Faversham (1900)	46	Later *Pride of Sheppey*	141
Ethel	Harwich	Cann Harwich (1894)	68		97
Ethel Edith	Ipswich then Faversham	Peck Ipswich (1892)	94		62,77
Ethel Maud	Maldon	Howard Maldon (1889)	45	Auxiliary fitted 1952	19,21,44,78
					108,129,142
Eva Annie	Maldon	Sittingbourne (1878)	45		38,100
Factor	Maldon	Bankside (8133)	48		83
Fairy	Rochester	Chatham (1864)	38		29
Falcon	Maldon	Kemp Paglesham (1868)	44		137
Fanny	Maldon	Taylor Murston (1872)	43		38,50,135
Favorite	Rochester	Sittingbourne (1803)	49	then 45, rebuilt 1898	108,120
Florence	Faversham	Murston (1858)	39		30
Formosa	Rochester	Rochester (1880)	42		88
Fortune				17th Century hoy	32
Four Brothers				Early 19th century hoy	82
Four Sisters	Faversham	Spencelaugh Sittingbourne (1877)	45		119
Frances	London	Rochester (1890)	44	Broken up 1957	88
Freston Tower	Ipswich	Cann Harwich (1889)	50	Houseboat 1950	36
Friends Increase	Maldon	Newbury (1835)	36		34
Friendship	Colchester	Taylor Crown Quay (1890)	207		27,101
Funf Gebruder	Maldon	Hanover (1842)	33		100
Garfield	Rochester	Smeed Dean Murston (1882)	38	Rebuilt 1920	106
Geisha	London	Braby Deptford (1898)	70		140

Name	Registered	Built	Tons	Remarks	Page
Genesta	Harwich	Vaux Harwich (1886)	99		47
George	Rochester	Smeed Dean Murston (1879)	47		108
George Cookson	London	Millbank (1865)	58		35,135
George & Eliza	Rochester	Rochester (1906)	56	Sank 19.4.1962 on West Mersea	142
George Smeed	Rochester	Smeed Dean Murston (1882)	59	Rebuilt 1922 at 64 ton; Unrigged 1955	106
Georgiana	Rochester	Smeed Dean Murston (1881)	46		122
Gladstone	Rochester	Rochester (1867)	38		92
Gladstone	Rochester	Smeed Dean Murston (1877)	41		89
Gladys	Rochester	Gill Rochester (1897)	50		136,137
Gleaner	London	Limehouse (1897)	28		119
Glenbury	Rochester	Little Rochester (1907)	64		146
Glencoe	London	Prince Edward Isle (1864)	132	Schooner	83
Gold Belt	Faversham	Gill Rochester (1892)	43	Ex *Orion*	23,40,47,77,138
Golden Fleece	Colchester	Gill Frindsbury (1903)	50		62
Goldfinch	Faversham	Goldfinch Faversham (1894)	117		44,62,133
Good Intent	London	Chelsea (1790)	44		92
Good Intent	Ramsgate	Faversham (1805)	44	Hoy	23,32
Good Templar	Rochester	Sittingbourne (1877)	41	Rebuilt 1899	60
Godwit	Rochester	Shrubsall Sittingbourne (1882)	50		136
Graham	Rochester	Smeed Dean Murston (1897)	37	Derelict Kingsnorth 1950	108
Grange				Lighter	137
Gratitude	Faversham	Shrubsall Sittingbourne (1880)	38		79
Grebe	Rochester	Letley Halstow (1890)	44		87
Greenhithe	London	Fellows Yarmouth (1923)	89		42
Gwynronald	London	East Greenwich (1908)	85	Ex *Charles Allison*. Renamed 1917	44
Hannah	London	Woolwich (1831)	35		38
Harmony	Faversham	Redman Faversham (1825)	23		36,103
Harmony	Faversham	Redman Faversham (1857)	25		103
Helvellyn	Rochester	Masters Sittingbourne (1884)	49		100
Henry	London	Goldsmith Grays (1904)	44		149
Henry Wood	Rochester	Sittingbourne (1877)	43		147
Hereford	London	Eastwoods Sittingbourne (1907)	33		136
Hero	Faversham	Sittingbourne (1811)	40		100
Histed	Rochester	Ipswich (1880)	53		50,106
Hope	Maldon	Limehouse (1820)	38		82
Hope	Faversham			Early 19th century hoy	103
Hope		(1854)			147
Hope	Rochester	Blackwall (1881)	45		50
Hopewell	Maldon	Pangbourne (1803)	35		93
Hyancinth	Maldon	Howard Maldon (1889)	45		19
Hydrogen	London	Gill Rochester (1906)	98	Auxiliary 1941	89,124,125
Ibis	Faversham	P.E.I. (1875)	195	Brigantine	28
Ida	Ipswich	Peck Ipswich (1895)	48		117,118
Imperial	London	Shrubsall East Greenwich (1902)	53	Motor barge 1949	47
Industry	Faversham	Southwark (1811)	14		103
Invicta	Rochester	Lee Halling (1867)	40		88
Invicta	Rochester	Shrubsall Sittingbourne (1877)	46		136
Iota	London	White Conyer (1898)	39		54,138
Ironsides	London	Clarke & Stanfield Thurrock (1900)	78	Engine fitted 1938	12,52,77,117
Jachin	Maldon	Howard Maldon (1893)	70	See *Venta*	144,145

Name	Registered	Built		Tons	Remarks	Page
James	Maldon		Lambeth (1846)	43		38,83
James	Maldon		Sittingbourne (1868)	48		38
James & Ann	Faversham	White	Conyer (1903)	42		44
James & Harriet	Maldon	Smee	Maldon (1864)	50		124 to 128
Jane	London		Sittingbourne (1893)	57		66,87
January	Rochester	Taylor	Sittingbourne (1868)	36		89
J.D. Drake	Rochester	Masters	Sittingbourne (1898)	40		100
Jess	Maldon	Howard	Maldon (1899)	49		126
Jesse	Maldon		Rochester (1867)	45		125
Jessie	Rochester	Smeed Dean	Murston (1888	42	Rebuilt 1916. Stranded 1922, C.T.L.	42,51
John Bayly	Ramsgate	Felton	Sandwich (1895)	56	Sank 1902, raised.	133
John Byford	London		Bow (1881)	39	Broken up, 1962	48
John & Edward	London	Taylor	Murston (1865)	43		41
John Evelyn	London		Deptford (1885)	72	Bombed	87
John & Mary	Faversham	White	Sittingbourne (1897)	45		54,55,117,138
John Ward	Rochester	Burham B.L.&C. Co	Sittingbourne (1871)	123		44
Joy	London	White	Conyer (1914)	56		83
J.S.H.	Rochester		Blackwall (1877)	40		50
Juliet	London	White	Sittingbourne (1896)	105		33
July	Rochester	Richardson	Boston (1869)	37		100
June	Rochester	Taylor	Murston (1869)	35		89
Kalulu	London	Gill	Rochester (1878)	36	Roads barge 1947	88
Kappa	London	White	Conyer (1898)	39		138
Katherina	London		Stadskanaal (1910)	91	Condemned 1939. Broken up Gravesend 1949	100
Keeble	Maldon	Shrubsall	Sittingbourne (1876)	46		38,135
Kent	Faversham		Rochester (1787)	88	Hoy	34,103
Kent	Faversham	Goldfinch	Faversham (1875)	27		34
Kimberley	Ipswich	Cann	Harwich (1900)	65		146
Kingfisher	Rochester		Maidstone (1899)	46		136
Kismet	London	Braby	Deptford (1899)	73		140
Kitty	Harwich	Cann	Harwich (1895)	65	Unrigged 1955	67,97,109,145
Lady Flora	London		Sittingbourne (1866)	36		45
Lady Gwynfred	London	Glover	Gravesend (1904)	88		12,44,112 114,144,153
Lady Helen	London	Gill	Rochester (1902)	56		42,52,142
Lady Jean	Rochester	Short	Rochester (1926)	87		133
Lapwing	London	Letley	Halstow (1893)	44		87,138
Lapwing SS					Steamer	77
Lena	Swansea		(1878)		Barquentine	28
Leofleda	Colchester	Cann	Harwich (1914)	48	Sank recently in Caribbean	142
Leslie	Rochester	Smeed Dean	Murston (1894)	43		59
Leslie West	London	Glover	Gravesend (1902)	57	Engine fitted 1949	137
Levetta					See *Murston*	
Livingstone	Rochester	Smeed Dean	Murston (1880)	48		119
Lizzie	Faversham		Sittingbourne (1867)	43		36
Llandudno	London	Wills & Packham	Sittingbourne 1892	43		136
Lord Lansdowne	London	Harveys	Clymping (1890)	109	Later Welsh owned and hulked at Falmouth	58,59,77
Lord Nelson	Faversham	White	Conyer (1898)	45	Sunk in collision	62

Name	Registered	Built		Tons	Remarks	Page
Remercie	Harwich	Maclearon	Harwich (1908)	67		109,142,143
Repertor	Harwich	Horlock	Mistley (1924)	69		11,30,75,76,77,140
Resourceful	Harwich	Horlock	Mistley (1930)		Converted to full power 1933	76
Resolution					Early 19th century hoy	34
Rettendon	Maldon	Shrubsall	Sittingbourne (1868)	46		83,135
Richard					Late 18th century hoy	103
Ripple					Yawl	97
Roache	Maldon	Shrubsall	Sittingbourne (1867)	43	Broken up at Stoke Saltings	83,135
Robert Adamson	Maldon		Sunderland (1865)	159	Brigantine	44,47
Robert Powell			Borstal (1904)		Rebuilt Ipswich 1908 (See Wolsey)	79
Robin Hood	Maldon			60	Early 19th century hoy	34
Rochford					Late 18th century hoy	34,103
Rogue in Grain	Maldon		Maldon (1838)	45		100
Rosa	Rochester	Bird	Conyer (1878)	36		37
Rose	Maldon	Howard	Maldon (1880)	42	Unrigged 1936	19,26
Royal Oak	Maldon		Limehouse (1798)	59		23,83,84
Royal Frederick	Rochester		Faversham (1825)	45		23
Runwell	Maldon		Poplar (1834)	40		83
Russell	Rochester	Smeed	Sittingbourne (1879)	44	Rebuilt 1920	127,130
Ruth	Rochester		Rochester (1881)	40		40,41,47
Saint Brannock			Bideford (1838)	98	Barquentine	92
Saltcote Belle	Maldon	Howard	Maldon (1895)	89		19,27
Sam	Rochester	Smeed Dean	Murston (1895)	39		58,89
Sam Weller	London	White	Sittingbourne (1903)	46		132
Sara	London	White	Conyer (1902)	50		140
Sarah & Eliza	Faversham	Masters	Sittingbourne (1880)	36		102
Sarah & Helen	London		Battersea (1867)	54		83
Savoy	Dover		Rochester (1898)	69		78,125,142
Scone	Rochester		Rochester (1919)	74		142
Scot	London	Fay	Southampton (1898)	80		137,140
Scotia	London	Fay	Southampton (1899)	67		137,140
Scotscraig	Maldon		Dundee (1866)	240	Brig	125
Scotsman	London	Wills & Packham	Crown Quay (1899)	44	Rebuilt 1933 as 63 tons	101
Scout	London	Norton	East Greenwich (1905)	50		97
Scud	London	Norton	East Greenwich (1907)	64		97
S.D.	London	Smeed Dean	Murston (1902)	131		40,153
Sela	Faversham		P.E.I. (1859)	191	Brigantine	28
Serb	London	Norton	East Greenwich (1916)	75		97
Sidwell	Rochester	Mantle	Sittingbourne (1877)	48	then 44	108
Sigma	London		Ipswich (1898)	37	Damaged in collision 1936	87
Sirdar	London	Shrubsall	Ipswich (1898)	53		140
Sir Joseph Yorke					Paddle ship	84
Southwark	London		Greenwich (1901)	50	Became Roads barge in 1942	50,135
Speranza	London	Fay	Southampton (1899)	67		132
Spinaway C.	Ipswich	Orvis	Ipswich (1899)	57		21,139,140,144
Spurgeon	Rochester	Smeed Dean	Murston (1883)	46	Rebuilt 1924	106
Stourgate					Tanker	129
Sunbeam	Maldon	Howard	Maldon (1888)	45		38,43,100
Surprise	Maldon	Hoad	Sandwich (1852)	140	Schooner	125
Surprise	Maldon	Shrubsall	Sittingbourne (1864)	39	Sank 1922	82,125
Surprise	Maldon	Howard	Maldon (1879)	44	Derelict Queenborough 1935	25,38,82

Name	Registered	Built		Tons	Remarks	Page
Suffolk					See *Mid Kent*	
Surrey	London	Eastwoods	Sittingbourne (1903)	34	Derelict 1938	88,90
Tartar	Maldon		Maldon (1793)	11	Boomsail	100
Thalatta	Harwich	McLearon	Harwich (1906)	67		142
Theresa	London	White	Sittingbourne (1892)	92	Later *Theresa Wood*	137
The Sisters	Maldon		Blackwall (1863)	33		38,137
Thistle	London	Hamilton	Port Glasgow (1895)	79	Rebuilt as motor barge 1949	100,142
Thistle	Colchester	Taylor	Crown Quay (1887)	137	Sold to France. Later *Jacques*	101
Thoma II	Maldon then Rochester	Howard	Maldon (1909)	67	Barge yacht	100
Thomas					17th century hoy	32
Thomas	Maldon		Pimlico (1851)	43		125
Thomas & Ann	Maldon		Southwark (1838)	41		38
Thomas & Frances	Rochester	Spencelaugh	Crown Quay (1878)	41		101,105
Three Sisters	Maldon	Smee	Maldon (1865)	47		125
Thyra	Rochester	Hutsons	Maidstone (1913)	62		77,142,143
Tish					No details known	124
Tit Bits	Ipswich	Orvis	Ipswich (1901)	23		126
Tollesbury	Ipswich	Felton	Sandwich (1901)	70		77,78,142
Triumph					Later *Coombdale*	
Trotter	London	Kemp	Paglesham (1875)	45		41
Trojan	London	Fay	Southampton (1898)	79	Became lighter, was rerigged 1940, motorised 1950	140
Two Friends	Maldon	Shrubsall	Sittingbourne (1865)	44		38,125
United Service					Tug	47,55
Unity	Maldon	Shrubsall	Sittingbourne (1871)	44		38,135
Uplees	Faversham	Dan	Faversham (1897)	39		98,99
Varuna	London	Shrubsall	East Greenwich (1907)	59	Sank recently down Channel	42,52,82 142
V.C.	London		Murston (1898)		Rebuilt 50 tons Ex *Donald*	106,108
Venta	London				Ex *Jachin*. Rebuilt Shrubsall, East Greenwich	19,60,100,134
Venture	London		Ipswich (1900)	58		67,140,144
Veravia	London	White	Sittingbourne (1898)		Ex *Alarm*. Rebuilt Shrubsall, East Greenwich 1925. 72 tons	76,140 143
Veronica	London	Shrubsall	East Greenwich (1906)	54	Now *Veronica Belle*	140
Vickers	Rochester		Southwark (1841)	36		83
Victa	Rochester		Rochester (1874	43	C.T.L. 1939 Ex. *& Co.*	136
Victoria	London	White	Sittingbourne (1897)	54		141
Vigilant	Harwich		Ipswich (1904)	68	then 76	143
Vincent	Rochester		Murston (1879)	35		106
Vicunia	London	Shrubsall	East Greenwich (1912)	75		110
Violet	Rochester	Bird	Teynham (1884)	42		147
Violet	Maldon	Howard	Maldon (1889)	45		19,100
Volante	London		Limehouse (1862)	25		88
Waterloo	Rochester		Millwall (1816)	44		83
Wave	Rochester		Chiswick (1851)	31		89
Westmoreland	London	White	Conyer (1900)	43	Wrecked 1973	19,87,95,114 115,131,139,140,153
Whaup	London	Letley	Upchurch (1892)	39		87,88
Why Not?	Faversham	Usher	Faversham (1866)	44		28,50
Wilfred	London	Piper	East Greenwich (1926)	98		133

Name	Registered	Built		Tons	Remarks	Page
Will Everard	London	Fellows	Yarmouth (1925)	150		55,90,142,143
William & Arthur	Maldon	Shrubsall	Sittingbourne (1869)	49		38,135
William Bennett	Rochester	Curel	Frindsbury (1875)	42		29
William Cleverly	Rochester	Co-operative Barge Building Society	Borstal (1899)	46		128,129,132 134,135
William Levett					Later *Emily Lloyd*	
William & Lucy	Maldon		St Osyth (1846)	51	Schooner	125
William & Lucy	Maldon	Smee	Maldon (1860)	48		125,127
William & Rebecca	Maldon		London (1825)	43		124
William & Richard	Maldon	Shrubsall	Sittingbourne (1862)	45		126
Wiltshire	London	Eastwoods	Sittingbourne (1908)	33		136
Wolsey	Ipswich		(1908)	65	Ex *Robert Powell*. Rebuilt Pauls, Ipswich	79,145
Wyvenhoe	London		Wivenhoe (1898)	45		142
Xylonite	Harwich	Horlock	Mistley (1926)	68		30,75,140
Yampa	London	Fay	Southampton (1899)	69		130
Yarana	London	Fay	Southampton (1899)	69		140
Yieldsted	Rochester		Rochester (1870)	38		21,79,104 119 to 123
York	London	White	Halstow (1900)	42		136
Youngarth	Rochester	Smeed Dean	Murston (1913)	68		89,90,91,151
Young Jack	Rochester	Smeed Dean	Murston (1880)	48		106

Register of rigged barges

Register of motor yacht barges or barges understood to be under re-rigging

Anglia	*Jock	*Phoenician	†Alice May
Ardwina	*Kathleen	*Pudge	Beatrice Maud
Asphodel	*Kimberley	*Redoubtable	British Empire
*Cabby	*Kitty	*Remercie	Henry
Cambria	*Lady Daphne	*Reminder	†King
*Centaur	*Lady Gwynfred	Seagull II	Thistle
*C.I.V.	*Lord Roberts	Sir A.P. Herbert ex	†Marie May
*Convoy	Lyford Anna ex Cereal	Lady Jean	†Mousme
Cygnet	Marjorie	Spinaway C	†Tollesbury
*Dawn	May	*Thalatta	Victor
*David Gestetner ex Ethel	Mayflower	Thoma II	
*Edith May	Millie	Venture	
Ethel Ada	*Mirosa ex Ready	Verona	
Ethel Ada	*Northdown	*Vicunia	
*Ethel Maud	*Olive May	*Vigilant	
*Felix	*Orinoco	*Will ex Will Everard	
*Ironsides			

*denotes craft rerigged from
motor barge or lighter hulls in
recent years.

†deonotes cruising motor yacht
barges.

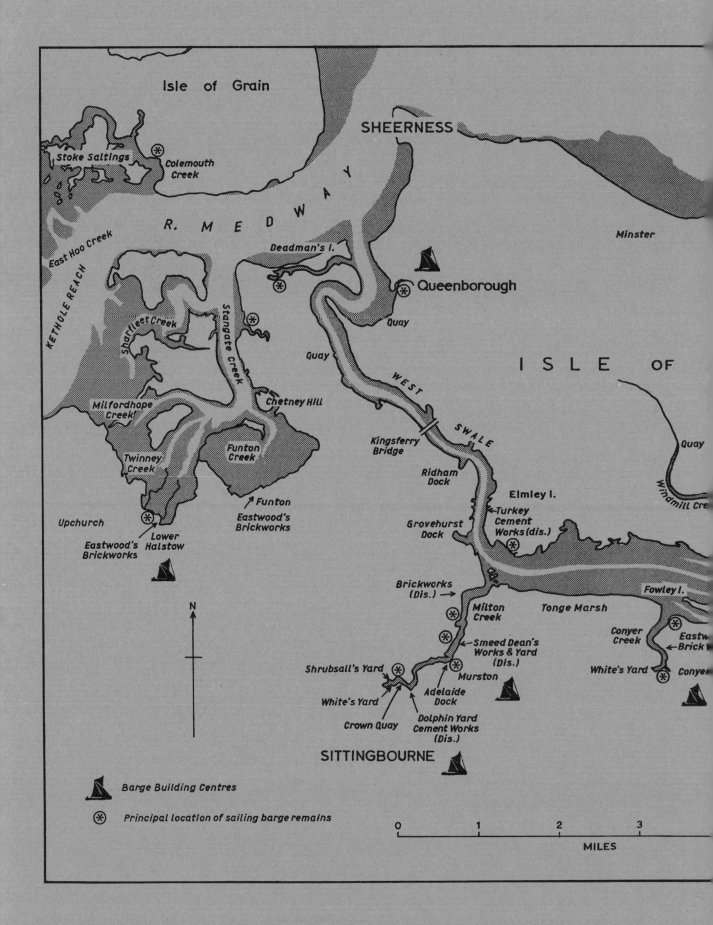

Isle of Grain

SHEERNESS

Stoke Saltings

Colemouth Creek

Minster

East Hoo Creek

R. MEDWAY

Deadman's I.

Queenborough

KETHOLE REACH

Sharfleet Creek

Stangate Creek

Quay

Quay

ISLE   OF

WEST

Milfordhope Creek

Chetney Hill

SWALE

Kingsferry Bridge

Quay

Twinney Creek

Funton Creek

Ridham Dock

Windmill Cre

Elmley I.

Funton
Eastwood's Brickworks

Grovehurst Dock

Turkey Cement Works (dis.)

Upchurch

Lower Halstow

Fowley I.

Eastwood's Brickworks

N

Brickworks (Dis.)

Milton Creek

Tonge Marsh

Conyer Creek

Eastw
Brick

Smeed Dean's Works & Yard (Dis.)

White's Yard

Conyer

Shrubsall's Yard

Murston

White's Yard

Adelaide Dock

Crown Quay

Dolphin Yard Cement Works (Dis.)

SITTINGBOURNE

Barge Building Centres

Principal location of sailing barge remains

0   1   2   3

MILES